The First Six Presidents under the Constitution

Bob Navarro

2014

Dedicated to my angel, Espy

Contents

The Foundation

The Establishment of the Presidency

The delegates of the First Continental Congress that met in September 1774 elected Peyton Randolph of Virginia as President to preside over the proceedings. The Congress also formed a Continental Association that became the first constitution of the United States. When Peyton Randolph resigned as President of the Congress, Henry Middleton of South Carolina was then elected to succeed Randolph to serve the remainder of Randolph's term of office. The sessions were significant in that the colonies acted together as the first formal government, and because the chief executive of the Congress marked the beginning of the United States Presidency.

The Second Continental Congress that convened in May 1775, again elected Peyton Randolph to be the chief executive of the Congress. When Peyton Randolph again resigned from the office, the Congress chose John Hancock of Massachusetts as its next President. Hancock and the delegates of Congress thus became the chief architects for the beginnings of the American government as they dealt with the powers of a central government and their relationship to each of the colonial governments. The Declaration of Independence became the basis for organizing the new government and served as the second constitution of the United States.

The Articles of Confederation that were ratified in 1781 served as the third constitution of the United States, and established the definition of the Congressional government into its executive, legislative and judicial components. When John Hanson was chosen to be President of the Congress in November 1781, he became the first official President of the nation under the Articles of Confederation. The powers and responsibilities of the executive branch of the United States Government were defined, with the Confederation Congress acting as a balance to ensure the freedom of the inhabitants of the United States. Although the executive branch was not a separate and independent entity, it still was the governing position, especially when the Congress was not in session.

The Constitution of the United States that was ratified in 1788 became the fourth constitution of the United States. It separated the government into 3 branches: executive, legislative and judicial, and established the rules under the Electoral College for choosing the President and Vice President of the United States. Although these executives are not chosen directly by the vote of the people, the selection was made according to the number of electoral votes as determined by their representation in Congress: the number of Senators and Representatives.

The rules that govern the Presidency are defined in the Constitution. The powers granted to the President by the Constitution include being in charge of all the armed forces to protect the people against foreign and domestic violence, the power to approve or veto legislation, the making of treaties with other sovereign nations, and the appointment of ambassadors, judges and officers of the executive department. It is an office that is almost untouchable from all judicial actions, except that a President is subject to impeachment by the Congress for conviction of a high crime such as treason or for a misdemeanor as interpreted by the Congress.

The Evolution of the Office

The Constitution was only an approved document when George Washington became President of the United States in 1789. Through his actions and those of the next 5 Presidents, the Constitution was transformed into an actualized process for conducting the business of government. Over this 40-year period the duties and powers of the President were extended beyond what was explicitly stated by the Constitution. The area of executive authority was expanded by implication into areas in which the Constitution was silent or vague. In the process, each of these Presidents established rules, customs and traditions according to their style of leadership.

George Washington began the process by expanding the executive framework. John Adams continued in the process by his appointment of John Marshall as Chief Justice of the Supreme Court—an action that resulted in the Supreme Court being elevated to an equal status with that of the Congress and the President. Thomas Jefferson began an informal style of government, attacked the Muslim pirates in a show of strength for the new national power, and doubled America's land area through his purchase of the Louisiana Territory—an action that went beyond the written powers of the Presidency. James Madison enhanced America's power in foreign policy concerns, including leading the War of 1812 with Great Britain. James Monroe formulated the foreign policy of opposition to European re-colonization of the American continent: the Monroe Doctrine. John Quincy Adams began a program of internal improvements, and started the Presidential opposition to the practice of slavery.

Only 2 Amendments to the Constitution were passed in this 40-year period. The Eleventh Amendment prevented suits from being brought by one state—or citizens of one state against another state. The Twelfth Amendment altered the manner in which the chief executive was chosen by having separate Electoral College votes for President and Vice President. Thus, the challenges and unrelenting pressures for these early Presidents were mostly those with regard to impediments and constraints placed on the office by judicial and legislative actions. These actions were what transformed the Constitution into an actualized reality instead of it just being a document. In the 40-year period from George Washington to John Quincy Adams, the government—and the Presidency—became firmly established through their combined legal precedents that they established.

The First United States Congress

The Makeup of the Congress

The First Congress had 11 Senators and 9 Representatives who had been involved in the framing of the United States Constitution. 18 Senators and 36 Representatives served in the Continental Congress. 4 of its members signed the Declaration of Independence, and one of them had been involved in every major document, from the Continental Association in 1774 to the Constitution in 1787. 2 of the members had been former Presidents of the Continental Congress. 3 of the members acted as Chairmen of the Committee of the Whole in the Continental Congress. Various members of both the House and Senate served in state positions, including those of administrators, jurists and legislators. Some were members of state conventions that were involved in writing state constitutions, or in ratifying the United States Constitution. Many had also been officers in the Continental Army. 2 of these members would become future Presidents of the United States.

The Senate

March 1789

- In March 1789, only 8 of 22 senators from the 11 states assembled in the new Senate at Federal Hall in New York City. The attendance was recorded, and since a quorum was not present, the Senate adjourned. More Senators arrived, but it was not until April 1789 that a quorum was achieved.
- John Langdon was elected as President of the Senate in March 1789 to preside over the sessions. As the leader of the Senate, and because the President, Vice President and Speaker of the House had not been sworn in yet, he became the first interim executive of the government, with his first duty being to open and count the Electoral College votes for President and Vice President of the United States.
- When the members of the House were in attendance at the Senate, Langdon opened and counted the votes that had been cast for President and Vice President. George Washington received 69 votes, thereby making him President of the United States, and John Adams received 34 votes, thus making him Vice President.

April 1789

- The Senate notified Washington and Adams of their election as President and Vice President.
- Rules were prepared for meetings in cases of conference between the Senate and the House. Rules were also prepared and approved for the meetings in which the Senate would conduct its own business.
- A Judiciary Committee was formed to deal with the creation of a federal court system. A judicial structure was devised and an intricate system of

interrelationships were defined between the federal and state courts as a shared sovereignty arrangement. The state judiciaries would be independent except to observe national laws, and would be protected by a framework of concurrent jurisdictions and systems of appeals. The decisions of the highest state courts would be final unless the matter was one of federal jurisdiction, or in a case that could be appealed to the United States Supreme Court.

- Vice President Adams addressed the Senate members. He congratulated the people of America for the formation of the Constitution and for the creation of a fair government under laws.
- The rules for communication and for the handling of a bill from the House to the Senate were instituted.
- Robert Livingston, the Chancellor of the State of New York, was chosen to administer the oath of office of President to George Washington.

The House of Representatives

March 1789

The new Federal Congress had been ordained by the old Continental Congress to meet in March 1789 as the new government. In March 1789, 13 of the 59 Representatives who had been elected from 11 states assembled in the new House of Representatives in Federal Hall in New York City. Since a quorum was not present, the House adjourned. More members arrived, but a quorum was not achieved until April 1789, when 30 members were present.

April 1789

- The first Speaker of the House, Frederick Muhlenburgh, was chosen by the attending Representatives. As the leader of the House of Representatives, and because the President and Vice President had not been sworn in yet, he became the second interim executive of the government. His duties would be to preside over the sessions, preserve the decorum of the assembly, decide on points of order, announce the results of votes by its members—including himself—and to appoint committees consisting of up to three members.
- The House appointed an 11-member committee to prepare the rules of procedure and order for the meetings of the Representatives. Four sections of rules were devised along with an oath to be taken by every member of the House. The Chief Justice of the State of New York administered the oath to each member.
- The House resolved itself into a Committee of the Whole with John Page of Virginia as Chairman. This was for the purpose of imposing duties on imports for goods, wares and merchandise brought into the United States, such as rum, molasses, wine, tea, spices, coffee and cocoa. James Madison from Virginia introduced the proposal for specified duties on certain articles. He saw the urgent need to raise operating revenue for the new government. In deference to public opinion that might not be ready for such a measure, Madison suggested that the tax be a temporary and limited one. However, many Representatives objected to a

temporary and limiting bill, citing the protection of domestic manufactures and the encouragement of production within the country as vital factors for a tariff to be enacted. Thus, the consideration of this impost raised a lot of debate among the members of the House. The bill was deemed to be critical, especially since it was designed as a necessity to deal with both the foreign and domestic debts. Thus, the bill for import duties became the first great controversial issue of the new government.

- More members arrived and took their seats in the House. More rules were considered and approved to provide the guidance for communications of papers, bills and messages, for holding conferences, and for proceedings requiring mutual agreements with the Senate. A Sergeant-at-Arms was appointed to execute the commands of the House as directed to by the Speaker of the House. He was the custodian of the mace—a symbol of authority with which he would restore order if the sessions became unruly. A clerk for the House was also appointed.

- The House discussions on the matter of duties being imposed on imports were made with much reference to the taxes that were imposed by the old Continental Congress in 1783. The debate also centered as to what constituted a luxury versus a necessity, and on what rates of taxation were to be charged for each type of article. These discussions were held on the matter of import duties with regard to hardships and inequalities as well as to raw materials versus manufactured items. The debates were very carefully argued to avoid the passing of any measure that would be viewed as unjust or unfair, especially in light of the recent travails that had been experienced to rid the country of tyranny and oppression. There was a great reluctance by various members to tax the poor for fear that it would create much discontent among the public.

- There was a consideration of restraint in taxing people of foreign nations coming into American ports because of the potential for retaliation by these nations to do the same for American ships going into their home ports. Yet, a policy of discrimination that would be favorable to foreigners as compared to the taxation of Americans might be a matter of great concern to the domestic population—even if great advantages were to be gained by reciprocity of friendship with foreign nations. A further complication was in showing a preference to vessels of one nation over those of another nation. In addition, there were the matters of how the tax bill was going to be enforced, on how smuggling was going to be prevented, and on the possibility of corruption by contraband trade and exposure of customs officers to temptation. Finally, the House realized that whether or not these import duties produced enough revenue to support the Government, it was a method that was to be preferred since recourse to excise or direct taxes could certainly not produce any more money.

- Upon the petition from David Ramsay the House took up the matter to consider copyrights. Another petition by John Churchman for the protection of maps was added to the issue of copyrights and the right of publishing. Still another petition was received by the House from mechanics and manufacturers of the city of New York. They wanted the restoration of trade and manufacturing to be established by allowing a list of items to be manufactured within the state of New York.

- President Washington agreed to take the oath in the House chamber, and then to move to the Senate chamber to deliver his address.
- A committee was formed to deal with the disposition of the papers from the former Secretary of the old Continental Congress, Charles Thomson.

George Washington

The First President Under the Constitution

Early Years

George Washington was born in Westmoreland County, Virginia on February 22, 1732. His father was Augustine Washington and his mother was Mary Ball. In 1743, George Washington's father died, and the estate was left to his half-brother. Raised by his mother, his formal education was slight and he was mostly concerned with plantation life and farming. He undertook self-studies in mathematics, writing and English history as well as surveying. He made a very good income from being a surveyor, and as a result of this activity he was able to buy many tracts of valuable land.

In 1751, he was commissioned as a surveyor for Culpepper County, Virginia. During this year he went on a trip to Barbados Island, a place where he had hopes of recuperating his health and healing the lung disease that he was suffering from. Instead, George Washington contracted smallpox, a disease that forever left his face pockmarked—but which also left him with a lifelong immunity against the malady.

When his half-brother died in 1752, George Washington inherited the estate of Mount Vernon and the mansion. He became District Adjutant for Southern Virginia, and became a Major because of that position. He began to read books on military tactics and through the Adjutant office he learned about politics.

Early Military Campaigns

In 1754, Washington was appointed as a Lieutenant Colonel by Governor Dinwiddie, and was sent as part of an expedition to defend a British outpost in the Ohio Territory. Washington won his first encounter with a French detachment and became the leader of the expedition with the rank of Colonel. In his next encounter with the French, Washington's troops were defeated at Fort Necessity and were forced to surrender. Under the terms of the capitulation, Washington and his garrison were allowed to return to their homeland. On his return, he was placed under the command of Colonel James Innes, and he was forced to resign his commission as Colonel.

In 1755, Washington rejoined the British army as a Captain. Captain Washington advised General Braddock of a plan to advance into French territory that General Braddock agreed to put into action. However, the British were attacked by the French, with General Braddock being severely wounded. Washington was able to retreat with the wounded General Braddock and what was left of his troops although General Braddock died on the way home.

Governor Dinwiddie offered Washington the post of Commander of the Virginia Regiment. Washington was also elected to the Virginia House of Burgesses in June 1758. Washington participated in a disastrous venture against the French ordered by General

John Forbes that ended in defeat of the English troops in the Ohio Territory. General Forbes sent another expedition in which Washington was in charge of 1 of 3 brigades. At Fort DuQuesne the English took over the burned and abandoned post of Fort Duquesne and renamed it Fort Pitt. Washington reconsidered his command, and in 1758, he resigned his commission.

The Virginia Legislature

Washington returned to farm at his mansion at Mount Vernon, Virginia. In 1759, he married Martha Dandridge Curtis. He grew tobacco, wheat, flax and hemp, and he acquired more land. Washington served in the Virginia House of Burgesses from 1759 to 1768. When Governor Baron de Botetourt dissolved the Virginia House of Burgesses in 1768, Washington joined Peyton Randolph and other members of the House at the Raleigh Tavern in Williamsburg, Virginia to form an Association to create an agreement of nonimportation of British goods and nonexportation of American products. In 1769, Washington was reelected to the Assembly that convened once again.

Governor John Murray Earl of Dunmore dissolved the House of Burgesses once more in 1774. Again the ousted Burgesses met at Raleigh Tavern in Williamsburg, Virginia where they acted on resolutions presented by Richard Henry Lee. One of the recommendations from the Committee of Correspondence was to appoint deputies from the various colonies to meet at an annual congress to deliberate on measures for the united interests of America. At a convention of the ex-Burgesses that was held at Alexandria, Virginia in 1774, Washington was chosen as a delegate to the First Continental Congress.

First Continental Congress

Washington attended the Congress that was held at Carpenters' Hall in 1774 in Philadelphia, Pennsylvania. He did not write or speak at the Congress, but he did interact with the members of the Congress to learn about the issues that were confronting the colonists. At the end of the Congress, he signed the petition to the King of England in 1774, asking for a redress of grievances for the colonists. He also signed the agreement to create the Continental Association.

Interim Period

When the First Continental Congress adjourned in 1774, Washington returned to his home in Virginia. At another Virginia convention Washington was elected to attend the Second Continental Congress that was to be held in 1775. Washington was assigned to the committees that were to draw up a plan for the arming of men and to prepare a plan to develop the resources for war.

Second Continental Congress

Washington attended the Second Continental Congress in May 1775. He was on a committee concerned with the defense of New York, and on another committee concerned with supplying the colonies with ammunition and supplies. He was also on a committee that dealt with raising the money for the Continental Army, and was on another committee that drafted the rules and regulations for this army. Although he voted for reconciliation with England, he still continued to plan for a potential conflict. In June 1775, he was selected by the Second Continental Congress as Commander-in-Chief of the Continental Army.

Revolutionary War Campaign

In June 1775, General Washington left the Second Continental Congress to take command of the Continental Army located at Cambridge, Massachusetts. General Washington also had to undertake the task of introducing discipline and subordination to an army without order, unity or a well-defined leadership. He trained the troops while awaiting a major attack by the British Army who commanded the Boston area. He divided the assembled army of 14,500 men into 3 divisions consisting of 2 brigades each.

In October 1775, General Washington experienced the first major act of treason when Dr. Benjamin Church, the Director General of the Hospitals, was discovered to be in communication with the British. Dr. Church was tried and found guilty of treason, was dismissed from the army, and was thrown in jail[1]. In June 1776, General Washington experienced the second major traitorous act when Thomas Hickey was found to be part of a conspiracy against him. The plot involved an assassination attempt against General Washington and other high-ranking officers of the Continental Army. Hickey was tried, found guilty, and sentenced to be hanged.

In 1776, in the Battle of Long Island, the Continental Army under General Israel Putnam suffered losses numbering 200 men killed and 1000 men captured—including General John Sullivan. Despite being heavily outnumbered and outmaneuvered, General Washington suffered only minor damages in retreating his forces from Brooklyn Heights. In the Battle of Kips Bay, General Washington retreated further to Harlem Heights. There, at the Battle of Harlem Heights, General Washington's forces succeeded in halting the advance of the British. In October 1776, General Washington evacuated his forces from Manhattan and moved northward to White Plains. There he was attacked by the British—an action that caused General Washington to retreat further to North Castle in November 1776, then into Trenton, New Jersey, and finally across the Delaware River into Pennsylvania in December 1776.

In December 1776, General Washington led a raid across the Delaware River back into Trenton, New Jersey. His troops surprised the garrison of 1,400 Hessian soldiers of whom 900 were captured. This marked his second victory against the British. General Washington drove back the British and inflicted heavy losses at the Battle of Princeton in January 1777. Then he retreated to his winter quarters at Morristown, New Jersey.

In September 1777, General Washington's Army was defeated by the British at the Battle of Brandywine, and he was forced to withdraw his forces towards Philadelphia, Pennsylvania. In October 1777, General Washington's army was defeated at the Battle of Germantown in Pennsylvania forcing him to withdraw his forces to Whitemarsh. In December 1777, Washington moved from Whitmarsh and made his winter quarters at Valley Forge, Pennsylvania where his troops endured a very harsh and bleak winter.

In June 1778, at the Battle of Monmouth, General Washington's army was successful and occupied New York again. In December 1778, General Washington established his winter headquarters at Middlebrook, New Jersey. By May 1779, the ranks of his army had thinned considerably, and it was at this time that American General Benedict Arnold began to provide intelligence about General Washington's movements to the British Army.

Washington's army suffered an even worse winter in January 1780. His troops spent the winter in the freezing woods while General Washington was quartered in a mansion at Morristown, New Jersey. In September 1780, General Arnold proceeded with his plans to turn over the American fort at West Point to the British. General Washington experienced the third major act of treason when the capture of British Major Andre exposed his plot. As a result, General Arnold was forced to flee and take refuge on the British warship the *Vulture*. In October 1780, Major Andre was hanged as a spy.

In December 1780, General Washington again quartered his troops at Morristown, New Jersey for another winter. In April 1781, General Washington's troops were again without food, clothing and pay. In August 1781, the British Army occupied Yorktown, Virginia where the American siege began in September 1781, against the 8,000 British troops that were there. In October 1781, General Washington's troops defeated the British Army at Yorktown, Virginia.

The Constitutional Convention of 1787

In May 1787, Washington was selected to attend the Constitutional Convention that met at Philadelphia, Pennsylvania. He was elected to preside over it, and served as President of the Constitutional Convention from May 1787 until it ended in September 1787. During the debates Washington was one of the strongest proponents of a balanced central government, with his preference being for a government consisting of 3 equal branches. He favored a strong central government at the expense of states' rights. He also did not favor a military government because he thought that war veterans would be a political threat.

Washington spoke only once from the floor—this in favor of the compromise amendment for 30,000 constituents per Representative. He wanted a President to be elected by the people, and a three-fourths vote to be required to overturn a veto by the President. When the Constitutional Convention ended, Washington and 38 other delegates signed the document and submitted it to the states for ratification. Washington favored its adoption because he knew that 13 separate sovereignties without a strong central government would end in anarchy.

Election of 1789

In 1788, the Confederation Congress prepared the procedures for choosing the electors for the President of the United States. In 1789, the first presidential election was held, and the results of the election were announced in the Senate. George Washington was chosen as President with 69 votes of those Electoral College representatives who participated.

The President of the Senate, John Langdon prepared a letter addressed to George Washington that was delivered by Charles Thomson. This was the formal notification to him that he had been elected as President of the United States. Washington accepted with a short speech, and prepared a letter to President Langdon of the Senate of his acceptance of the position. Then, he set out to travel to New York City to assume the duties of the Presidency.

Endnotes

1   Dr. Benjamin Church was held in prison until 1777, when he was released. He then sailed to the West Indies in exile. While en route, the ship that he was on sank and Dr. Church was lost at sea.

The First Term of George Washington

Events: 1789

April 1789

- In the first Inaugural Address, President Washington appealed to the populace to preserve the liberties and happiness of everyone. He wanted the conduct of a united government to proceed in a way that would benefit the people of the country with future blessings. He also appealed to the populace to conduct policies without regard to political party animosities, with honesty and magnanimous behavior. He wanted to preserve the freedoms that had been fought for—something that he felt would guide the country to its rightful destiny. In particular, he warned against altering the Constitution until enough experience had been gained to do so. He also warned against using the Presidency for gain and profit. He concluded by expressing his ideals and hopes for peaceful deliberations and unanimous decisions in everything that affected the people—especially in their pursuit of happiness in relationship to the conduct of government.
- President Washington began his duties from the first presidential residence located in New York City.
- The executive branch consisted only of President Washington and Vice President Adams. No cabinet existed yet since the departments of War, the Treasury and State had not yet been created by Congress.
- In July 1789, Congress passed an act to create the first executive department, that of Foreign Affairs—which in September 1789 was renamed as the Department of State. Thomas Jefferson was appointed by Washington to head this department—a position that became known as the Secretary of State.
- In August 1789, Congress created the War Department. Henry Knox was appointed by Washington to head the department—a position that became known as the Secretary of War, the predecessor of the Secretary of Defense.
- In September 1789, Congress created the Treasury Department, and Alexander Hamilton was appointed by President Washington to head the department—a position that became the Secretary of the Treasury.
- In September 1789, Congress created the office of Attorney General, and Edmund Randolph was appointed by President Washington to be the Attorney General.
- In September 1789, Congress created the position of Postmaster General to be under the Department of the Treasury, and Samuel Osgood was appointed by President Washington to serve as Postmaster General.

Events: 1789

May 1789

- House advocates for the imposition of duties on imports argued that it was a necessary sacrifice to pay for the national security.

- The House expressed its share of the obligation to carry out the system of legislation and to conduct its actions as dictated by the Constitution.
- James Madison introduced the Bill of Rights that was to be considered as the set of Amendments to the Constitution. From a total of 210 that had been submitted by the states, he was able to summarize these into 19 Amendments.
- The House began the creation of 3 executive departments—those of War, Foreign Affairs and the Treasury.
- The Senate pledged to work for the welfare of all, to divest themselves of prejudices and attachments, and to establish by its actions the foundation of national policy as one being based on private morality of each of its members.
- The Senate appointed a committee to consider a bill defining the crimes and offenses that would be considered as punishable under the authority of the United States.

June 1789

- Congress passed its first act: the administration of oaths for public office. Senator Langdon then administered the oath to Vice President John Adams who in turn administered the oath to the rest of the Senators. In the House, Speaker Muhlenburg administered the oath to all Representatives.
- The Senate reported on a bill to establish the federal judiciary system of the United States, and reviewed the House's bill for the establishment of the Executive Departments.

July 1789

- Congress passed its first Tariff Act to raise revenue by setting a protective rate of up to 50 percent on 30 different commodities, and a 5 percent rate tax on all other imports.
- Congress passed the Tonnage Act that instituted a tax on all foreign and American ships entering American ports. The tonnage duty on foreign ships was set to 50 cents per ton while those on American ships was set to 6 cents per ton.
- The House established a Committee of Ways and Means. The job of this committee was to review the finances of America and then to estimate the supplies that would be necessary to meet the demands for the current year. 10 members were chosen for the original committee.

August 1789

- President Washington asserted himself by establishing the custom of taking charge of foreign affairs entirely without Senate participation—including treaty making—and only leaving them the task of either acceptance or rejection after a treaty had been negotiated.
- The House approved 17 of the 19 amendments that had been submitted and sent them to the Senate for its review.

- The House conceded that it was the right of the President and the Senate to make treaties. However, it asserted its right to defray all expenses associated with such treaties, for example, to raise troops.
- President Washington chose Arthur St. Clair as Governor of the Western Territory.

September 1789

- Compensation for members of the executive branch and for members of Congress was established by a series of bills that were passed by the House and Senate. President Washington's salary was set at $25,000 per year to include all of his expenses. The salary of the Vice President was set at $5,000 per year. Members of Congress were to be paid $6 per day while they were in session, and $6 per day while traveling to and from Congress.
- Congress passed the Federal Judiciary Act to create the federal court system. President Washington appointed John Jay as the first Supreme Court Chief Justice in a court composed of 6 members.
- Congress created 13 federal district courts and 3 federal circuit courts, with the salaries for the Judges and the Attorney General being fixed at $3,500 per year.
- Congress submitted the 12 proposed Amendments to the Constitution—the Bill of Rights—for ratification by the states. 10 of these were ratified and added to the Constitution, thus becoming the Bill of Rights.
- Congress founded the United States Army consisting of a total of 1,000 soldiers structured as a single regiment composed of 8 infantry companies, and one battalion comprised of 4 artillery companies.

November 1789

- President Washington proclaimed the first national Thanksgiving Day that Congress had established by a resolution as a national holiday to offer thanks. It was celebrated in November 1789.
- The twelfth state ratified the Constitution.
- The first state ratified the proposed Amendments to the Constitution.

Events: 1790

January 1790

- President Washington addressed the Congress in the first State of the Union report.
- Alexander Hamilton presented the first report of the national debt to Congress—an amount equal to almost $80,000,000. This combined foreign, national and state debt had been accumulated by the Confederation Congress to fight the Revolutionary War. Hamilton also presented his plan for funding the debt through the use of federal securities.

- The Senate passed a bill defining the acts and punishments for offenses that were committed against the United States.

- The President's quarters were relocated to a residence in New York City.
- The House debated the rule of naturalization, public credit, and the slave trade, but the latter was tabled due to protests.

March 1790

- Congress passed the Census Act to count the number of inhabitants who were living in the United States. The count did not include Native Americans but did include whites, free blacks and enslaved blacks—although blacks were only counted as three-fifths of a white person.
- Congress passed a Naturalization Act that set a 2-year requirement of residency in the United States to qualify for citizenship.

April 1790

- Congress established the Revenue Marine Service as part of the Treasury Department, the predecessor of the Coast Guard that guards the coastlines of the United States to protect against illegal import and entry activities.
- Congress passed the first patent law.
- $19,300,000 in state debts was proposed to be assumed by the government.
- The House considered punishments for crimes committed against the United States, especially that of counterfeiting and forgery. Proposals were made for forfeitures and penalties under revenue laws. A tariff of duties was proposed listing a variety of goods on which levies were to be imposed.

May 1790

- The first Copyright Act was signed by President Washington to protect written materials for an initial period of 14 years. It included the right of renewal for another 14 years.
- The thirteenth state ratified the Constitution.
- The House rejected the assumption of state debts by the federal government.

June 1790

- The compromise to have the Federal Government assume the war debts of the states was worked out by Alexander Hamilton.
- The capital of the United States was moved to the banks of the Potomac River.
  July 1790
- The United States Patent Office was opened.

- The first census was completed, and it determined a population of almost 4,000,000 people in the United States. Philadelphia was the largest city with 42,000 inhabitants, followed by New York, Boston, Charleston and Baltimore. Virginia was the most populous state with 820,000 inhabitants.
- Congress passed the Funding Act that allowed the issuance of bonds to pay off the Revolutionary War debts. The Treasury department issued the bonds which would bear interest at the rate of 6 percent when due.

December 1790

- The President's quarters were moved to a residence in Philadelphia, Pennsylvania where President Washington.
- President Washington delivered his second State of the Union address to the Congress.
- Alexander Hamilton presented a plan for a Bank of the United States to assume the state debts. The bank was to have a capital of $10,000,000. The bank would handle the national debt and its money would act as a national currency.
- The House took up the issues of selecting the Electors of the Electoral College, and of filling the vacancies of the offices of President and Vice President in case of death, illness or other absence.
- The House worked on a bill to establish a uniform militia across the United States.

Events: 1791

January 1791

- Alexander Hamilton presented a plan to Congress for the establishment of a national mint.

February 1791

- President Washington signed the bill that established the charter for the First Bank of the United States.

March 1791

- The Federal district was chosen by President Washington to be by the Potomac River.
- Vermont became the fourteenth state to be admitted to the Union.
- Congress passed the Whisky Act that placed a tax on distilled liquors and the stills. It also established 14 revenue districts.

October 1791

- The House used the first census to establish the ratio of one Representative for every 30,000 inhabitants.

November 1791

- President Washington began the practice of having regular cabinet meetings to discuss domestic, foreign and military matters.
- The House took up the matter of imprisonment for debt to provide for a uniform rule and to establish a uniform system of bankruptcy laws for the United States.
- The Senate took up the issues for establishing the mint, fixing the standard of weights and measures, choosing the Electors of the Electoral College, providing compensation for the judiciary, the granting of lands, and establishing the fees for Consuls and Vice Consuls.

December 1791

- The eleventh state ratified the Bill of Rights, thus making the Ten Amendments to the Constitution into law.
- The First Bank of the United States opened its doors for business as the holder of gold and silver to back the American currency.
- The Secretary of Treasury, Alexander Hamilton, presented a plan to Congress for a tariff system to protect American goods, an agricultural bounty system to encourage farming, and a public works project to build roads and canals.
- The House started work on establishing post offices and postal roads within the United States.

Events: 1792

January 1792

- The Senate proceeded with outlining the specific sections of the Post Office bill in terms of duties, roads, offices and all other aspects of the postal system.

February 1792

- Congress passed the Presidential Succession Act to establish the successors to the President and the Vice President in case of removal, death, resignation or incapacitation. The President of the Senate and the Speaker of the House were designated as next in line to succeed the Vice President.
- Congress enacted a bill to regulate the processes of the federal courts.

April 1792

- Congress passed the Coinage Act to establish a Federal Mint at Philadelphia, Pennsylvania.

May 1792

- Congress passed the Militia Act to create the first military draft of men between the ages of 18 and 45.

June 1792

- Kentucky was admitted as the fifteenth state to the Union.

September 1792

- President Washington issued a proclamation warning against opposition to the Whisky Tax.

December 1792

- George Washington was reelected with 132 Electoral College votes.

Events: 1793

February 1793

- Supreme Court Justice John Jay ruled in *Chisolm v. Georgia* that a citizen from one state could sue another state in Federal Court. This ruling made American citizens equal in sovereignty with the United States.

The Second Term of George Washington

Events: 1793

March 1793

- Washington gave a very short Inaugural Address. He stated his intention to continue to guide the nation, and his appreciation of the honor bestowed upon him by the populace of a united America. President Washington then took the oath of office as administered by Judge Cushing of the Supreme Court.
- President Washington's executive branch was as follows:
  - Secretary of State Thomas Jefferson. In July 1793, Thomas Jefferson resigned as Secretary of State over his long running battle with Alexander Hamilton, but he decided to stay—at President Washington's request—until the end of December 1793. In January 1794, Edmund Randolph succeeded Thomas Jefferson as Secretary of State. In August 1795, Edmund Randolph resigned as Secretary of State. In December 1795, President Washington announced the selection of Timothy Pickering as his Secretary of State.
  - Secretary of the Treasury Alexander Hamilton. Alexander Hamilton resigned as Secretary of the Treasury and was succeeded by Oliver Wolcott, Jr.
  - Secretary of War Henry Knox. In January 1795, Henry Knox resigned as Secretary of War and was succeeded by Timothy Pickering. In January 1796, President Washington Chose James McHenry as Secretary of War.
  - Attorney General Edmund Randolph. In January 1796, President Washington nominated Charles Lee as Attorney General.
  - Postmaster General Timothy Pickering.

April 1793
- President Washington issued a Proclamation of Neutrality— a proclamation that declared that the United States would pursue a conduct friendly and impartial toward the belligerent nations.

November 1793

- A slave rebellion in Albany, New York resulted in devastating fires in that city.

December 1793

President Washington delivered his Fifth State of the Union Address in which he explained the reasons for the neutrality proclamation.

Events: 1794

January 1794

- Congress ordered the addition of 2 more stars and 2 more stripes to the American flag, making it have 15 stripes and 15 stars to represent the states of Vermont and Kentucky that had been admitted to the union.

March 1794

- Congress established the United States Navy.
- Congress submitted the Eleventh Amendment to the Constitution for ratification by the states. The Amendment repealed the clause in the Constitution that allowed a citizen of one state to sue another state.

May 1794

- The House proposed taxes on stamps, tobacco, sugar, coffee and cocoa to derive revenue.
- The Senate considered a bill to make further provisions for securing and collecting the whiskey tax.

June 1794

- Congress passed the Neutrality Act to enforce President Washington's proclamation.
- The House considered a bill for the punishment of crimes committed against the United States.
- The Senate enacted that the President be authorized to establish military posts and call up militias as necessary to protect the Southwestern frontier.

July 1794

- The Whisky Rebellion took place in Western Pennsylvania. In response, President Washington ordered a militia of 13,000 men to put down the insurrection.

August 1794

- President Washington issued the first proclamation that directed the insurgents in the Whiskey Rebellion to return to their homes.

September 1794

- President Washington issued a second proclamation, which ordered the suppression of the Whiskey Rebellion.

October 1794

- President Washington appointed General Henry Lee to lead the federal militia against the Whisky Rebellion.

November 1794

- The House established rules and orders for itself, including those of the duties of the Speaker, on decorum and debate, on the motions of introducing bills for discussion, in forming Committees of the Whole, and on joint conferences with the Senate.
- The House introduced a bill to allow the President to station troops in Western Pennsylvania for a limited amount of time.

December 1794

- The House considered a plan to reduce the public debt, which was over $6,000,000.

Events: 1795

January 1795

- Congress passed the Naturalization Act that mandated a 5-year residency in the United States to qualify for citizenship. The act also stipulated that the children of persons who had been naturalized would be extended citizenship rights, and further that any children of citizens who were born outside of the United States would also be considered as citizens.

February 1795

- The Senate concurred with the House on an act that allowed the calling of the militia to enforce the laws of the country, to suppress insurrections, and to repel foreign invasions.

July 1795

- John Jay resigned as Chief Justice of the Supreme Court, and President Washington nominated John Rutledge of South Carolina to replace him.

August 1795

- President Washington signed Jay's Treaty into law, thereby setting a precedent of executive prerogative. This affirmed the Constitution in that both houses of the Congress were not required to vote their agreement for the validation of a treaty.

- The United States signed a treaty of peace and amity with Algiers that included a payment of tribute of $1,000,000 to the Barbary Pirates in exchange for the return of 115 captured American seamen.

December 1795

- President Washington delivered his Seventh Annual Address to the Congress.
- The House agreed to joint rules and orders with the Senate.
- The House voted to create a permanent Ways and Means Committee.
- The Senate rejected the nomination of John Rutledge as Chief Justice of the Supreme Court. President Washington then nominated William Cushing as Chief Justice of the Supreme Court, but Cushing declined the job—after being confirmed by the Senate. In the interim, Associate Justice John Blair resigned.

Events: 1796

January 1796

- President Washington appointed Samuel Chase as Associate Justice on the Supreme Court, and appointed Oliver Ellsworth as Chief Justice.

March 1796

- The Supreme Court ruled in *Hyston v. United States* that a 1794 carriage tax was a valid indirect tax.
- The House put forth a constitutional challenge to the supporting documents concerned with Jay's Treaty that were in President Washington's possession. Washington, citing Constitutional privilege, declined to surrender these papers to the House.

April 1796

- The Supreme Court ruled that treaties made under the Constitution take precedence over state laws, and thus reaffirmed federal rights over state rights in cases of conflicting statues.
- The debt for the United States was calculated to be $18,400,000 for 1796, and later revised to $13,900,000.
- President Washington won over the Congress in his refusal to turn over papers, and set a precedent in terms of executive privilege.

May 1796

- Congress passed the Land Act to survey all public lands in the Northwest Territory and to permit the sale of these lands at public auctions. Congress set the minimum price at $2 an acre and the minimum tract at 640 acres.
- A bill to regulate a quarantine was considered by the House, but was objected to as taking away the power of a state to regulate the health of its citizens.

June 1796

- Tennessee was admitted as the sixteenth state to the Union.

September 1796

- President Washington published his Farewell Address in which he expressed the right of the American people to change their government. At the same time he stressed that the Constitution was obligatory as well. He warned against divisive party systems, permanent foreign alliances and an overly powerful military establishment.

November 1796

- The United States signed a treaty with Tripoli to seek a further end to the raids by the Barbary Pirates on American ships. Another large tribute was offered for imprisoned American sailors.

December 1796

- John Adams was chosen as President with 71 Electoral votes.
- In his eighth State of the Union Address to the Congress, President Washington spoke about the need for a national university to be based in the nation's capital as well as a military academy.

Events: 1797

February 1797

- The House established procedures for any future contested elections for a Representative.

March 1797

- George Washington completed his second term as President.
- John Adams took the oath of office of President as administered by Chief Justice Oliver Ellsworth.

Later Years

George Washington returned to his home at Mount Vernon, Virginia in 1797. He adhered to the principle of not making comments on the current government's affairs or its officers. He collected art, sold some of his land holdings to generate the needed income for his retirement, was involved with farming, and stayed involved in the projects concerning the federal city, the national university and the Potomac Canal.

In 1798, the threat of war with the French led President John Adams to call up a new federal army. The Senate approved of President Adam's selection of Washington as Commander-in-Chief of these forces. However, the threat of war subsided, and Washington returned once again to his home at Mount Vernon, Virginia. In December 1799, Washington developed a severe throat infection, and on December 14, 1799, George Washington died at the age of 67.

Legacy

As the first President under the Constitution, Washington established the Presidency by setting precedents and by using precedents that had been established by the Presidents of the Continental Congress. Through his decisions Washington created the framework for the United States and helped it to survive during its early years. This was especially true in keeping the nation together against the forces of insurrection.

President Washington and Congress established the first executive departments, and he built the foundation for the judicial branch. With the Congress he created the foundation for both the Navy and the Army. In financial matters, he followed policies that provided for adequate revenue, established a sound currency system, and created a federal banking structure. He was also responsible with Congress for launching a well-supported public credit business environment—including aid for both manufacturing and shipping. By his promotion of trade and revenue from tariff duties, Washington also enabled the United States to sustain its standing with respect to public credit and to meet all of its necessary obligations and expenses.

In foreign affairs Washington and Congress created the diplomatic service. He was determined to keep the nation from being involved in any more wars, and his proclamation of neutrality in 1793 for the United States kept the country from being a participant in the English-Franco War. He also dealt with Spain in a manner that allowed American settlers in the west to export their goods and to hold on to territories in dispute. He concluded a treaty with Algiers to protect American shipping in the Mediterranean Sea against attacks by the Muslim Barbary Pirates. Thus, he enabled the new government of the United States to take root by avoiding conflicts that might have shattered its structure before it had the necessary strength to survive. In his Farewell Address, Washington set in motion a policy of isolation from Europe—something that was observed by his successors for more than a century after his Presidency.

John Adams

The Second President Under the Constitution

Early Years

John Adams was born in Braintree, Massachusetts on October 31, 1735. His father, John Adams, was a shoemaker, selectman, farmer, and lieutenant in the local militia and deacon of the Puritan church. His mother was Susanna Boylston. He was taught to read at home, and then at a private school. He enjoyed swimming, fishing and shooting, and his wish was to be a farmer. However, his father insisted that he become a minister. Therefore, in 1750, he was admitted to Harvard where he was granted a partial scholarship. He studied mathematics and science, as well as logic, Latin and Greek. He graduated from Harvard in 1755.

But, Adams refused to become a minister. He taught at a grammar school at Worcester, Massachusetts where he began his study of law. Along with law books, he read many of the classics in English literature and some history texts. In 1759, he was admitted to the Massachusetts bar, and he began to practice law in Braintree. In 1761, his father died, and he inherited a substantial amount of property. His law practice picked up and he was involved with many cases in the Boston area. In October 1764, he was married to Abigail Smith.

Entry into Politics

His first political stance was that of opposition to the Stamp Act of 1765. He wrote an essay entitled *A Dissertation on the Canon and the Feudal Law*. In this essay he stated that American freedoms were not ideals to be obtained, but rather rights that were firmly established under British law. He also began writing articles in the *Boston Gazette* dealing with constitutional rights, and his original essay was published in 1765. In 1765, he printed the Braintree Instructions in the *Gazette*; these stated that no one should be subject to any tax that was enacted without his consent—no taxation without representation. This document was adopted by more than 40 towns, and marked one of the beginnings of the American Revolution.

In 1766, Adams was elected as a selectman in Braintree. In 1768, he moved to Boston, Massachusetts where he worked as an attorney. He was offered the office of Advocate-General by Governor Francis Bernard in the Court of Admiralty, but Adams refused to accept it since he would then not be free to oppose the policies of the English Crown.

In 1770, the Boston Massacre took place in which 5 American colonists were killed and 6 others were injured. He served as counsel for British Captain Preston in the first trial, and in a second trial for 8 of his soldiers who had been involved in the Boston Massacre. Preston and 6 of his soldiers were acquitted while the other 2 soldiers were found guilty of manslaughter.

In 1770, he was elected to the Massachusetts Legislature and became one of the leaders of the opposition. In 1772, he resigned his seat in the legislature, and wrote a series of very powerful articles on the threat to liberties of the colonists by the British Government. After the Boston Tea Party occurred in 1773, Adams proposed the impeachment of judges for high crimes and misdemeanors. When oppressive acts were passed by the British Parliament in 1774, Adams was chosen as a delegate to attend the First Continental Congress in Philadelphia, Pennsylvania.

First Continental Congress

John Adams attended the First Continental Congress in 1774. He was on a committee that prepared an address to the King of England. He wrote the fourth article of the Resolutions of the rights and grievances of the colonies, the one that advocated independence. In particular, Adams argued that the foundation of all free government is the right of the people to participate in their legislative council. He also excluded the idea of all taxation, whether external or internal, for raising revenue on the subjects of America without their consent. He was one of the 51 signers of the petition that was submitted to the King of England.

Second Continental Congress

John Adams attended the Second Continental Congress in 1775. He was convinced that matters had deteriorated to the point where reconciliation with Britain was impossible. He had been affected by the British actions at Lexington and Concord, and he knew that there was no use in sending any more petitions to the King.

Adams was appointed to serve on various committees, including those concerned with drafting the commissions and instructions for the Commander-in-Chief, George Washington, the Major Generals and the Brigadier Generals. He was also on a committee that was responsible for printing the first Continental currency—an amount equal to $2,000,000—with each Continental dollar being redeemable for a Spanish milled dollar. One of the most important committees that Adams was a member of was the one concerned with determining what steps needed to be taken for the preservation of liberties in America.

Adams left the Congress in 1775, but returned in 1776. He wrote *Thoughts on Government, Applicable to the Present State of the American Colonies* to assist North Carolina, South Carolina, Virginia and New Hampshire in formulating their state constitutions. In this document, Adams proposed 2 houses, an executive with the power of veto and an independent judiciary. Adams' foundation of government was based on equal representation by one assembly to represent the interests in an equal manner, and by representation that mirrored society in the other assembly to have an expression based on popular suffrage.

In 1776, the Continental Congress adopted the resolution by Adams that called for new constitutions in all of the states—the preliminary and decisive step towards separation from England. Adams was selected on a 5-man committee to write the document of independence. As chairman of the committee, Adams was originally chosen to draft the Declaration of Independence, but he deferred the task to Thomas Jefferson. Thus, in July 1776, by a vote of 12 colonies, Congress voted to declare independence. The document was presented before Congress, and again 12 colonies voted in the affirmative.

Adams served as Chairman on the Board of War, and he served on the foreign relations committee. He was instrumental in having Congress authorize a navy and privateers to fight the war, and was on a committee to prepare a plan for a military academy for the army. As a member of the Naval Committee, he drew up the rules for the navy that Congress adopted and published as official regulations. He also drafted the procedures for judicial trails in cases involving the capture of ships and their cargoes. And, he was on a committee whose task was to design a Great Seal for the United States of America.

Adams was involved in almost every debate in Congress, especially with those involved over the proposed Articles of Confederation. These were deemed important because Congress had no legal authority by which to make laws—it could only pass resolutions. Adams' concern over the Confederation was over the issue of voting: whether each colony would have only one vote or whether the number of votes of a colony would be in proportion to its population, wealth, exports and imports, or other factors.

In 1776, Adams was one of the persons who were chosen to meet with British Vice Admiral Richard Howe for peace negotiations. Although Adams mistrusted Lord Howe, he met with Lord Howe at Staten Island. The conversations proved fruitless since the Americans remained steadfast in their declaration of independence—something that Lord Howe wanted revoked. Adams returned to the Congress and formulated a set of Articles of War. He was also the first one to propose the creation of a military academy.

In 1776, he left the Congress once again, but returned in 1777. He was on a committee charged with determining the reward to be offered for destroying or taking ships of war and transports belonging to the enemy. He was also on a committee tasked with inquiring into the laws and customs of nations respecting neutrality. As chairman of the Board of War, he authorized General Washington to negotiate an exchange of prisoners with British General Howe. The Board of War also called out the militias of New Jersey, Pennsylvania, Delaware and Maryland to repel the invasion of the enemy.

In 1777, the Board of War made an urgent recommendation to the states for their help in providing clothing for the Army. Adams voted with the majority in Congress against the Ninth Article of Confederation that would have allowed each state to have one vote for every 50,000 inhabitants. He voted again with the majority in Congress against the Thirteenth Article that would have allowed each state to send one delegate to the Congress for every 30,000 inhabitants. Once more, he voted with the majority in Congress against the Ninth Article that would have allowed each state representation according to its contributions to the treasury. He also voted against the resolution that stated that each state in Congress would be represented by no less than 2 members or by no more than 7 members. In 1777, Adams left the Second Continental Congress after having served on over 90 committees, 25 of which he chaired.

Assignment in Europe

In November 1777, Adams was chosen to be the Commissioner to France. In 1778, Adams sailed to France aboard the frigate *Boston* to negotiate a treaty of alliance with the French. He arrived in Paris, France, and was presented to Louis XVI. Adams sought loans from both France and Holland, but he was unsuccessful in these endeavors. In 1779, Adams and others signed a letter stating that it was imperative for France to send a powerful fleet to American waters in order to secure naval superiority.

Adams sailed aboard the ship *Sensible* in 1779, and returned to Massachusetts. He wrote the new state constitution for Massachusetts with a plan for a governor with a power of veto, and 2 houses based on a government of law and the public good. A unique portion of this constitution had a section entitled "The Encouragement of Literature" as his plan to diffuse wisdom and knowledge to the general population for their use in the preservation of their rights and liberties. In 1779, Adams was re-appointed by Congress as one of the commissioners to negotiate a peace with England and to work on a treaty with Spain.

Adams sailed for France aboard the *Sensible* in November 1799. Adams mistrusted the French and he perceived that France was out to sacrifice the interests of the United States, and that her intervention on behalf of the Americans was purely selfish. In July 1780, Adams went to Holland to negotiate a loan of $2,000,000, to ask for diplomatic recognition for the United States and to arrange a treaty of friendship and trade. In 1781, he returned to Paris to continue work on the peace negotiations. Adams again inferred that the French were acting out of their own selfish means to prolong the war and weaken both the American colonies and England.

Adams returned to Amsterdam, Holland in 1781. When Holland recognized American independence in March 1782, Adams put out a flag at The Hague, the first American embassy, and thus became the very first United States Ambassador. In 1782, the $2,000,000 loan for the United States was granted by Holland.

Adams returned to Paris, France to continue with the peace negotiations. Adams argued for the right of Americans to be able to fish in the Atlantic Ocean. At the end of the negotiations, Adams rejected the claims of England that the Tories in America be compensated for their losses. Finally, the American treaty with the British was approved in 1782, and was ratified in 1783 by the Congress. Adams remained in France until 1784, and in 1785, Adams was appointed as Minister to England.

Ambassador to England

Adams set off for London in 1785, and met with King George III. Adams rented a house that became the first American legation in London. Adams' first priority was to open

British ports to American ships, but with an economy in shambles America was not taken seriously by the British. Although Adams met repeatedly with Prime Minister William Pitt, no answers were received to his many inquiries. In 1786, Adams was again dispatched to Holland to secure another loan for the United States. In 1786, he returned to his post as Ambassador to England. Adams resigned as Minister to England, and set sail for Boston in 1788, aboard the American ship *Lucretia*.

Vice President of the United States

In the first Electoral College election for President in 1788, Adams received 34 votes and became the first Vice President of the United States. Adams arrived in New York City in 1789, and was greeted by the Senate President *pro tempore*, John Langdon. Adams was involved in 31 tie votes in which he cast the deciding vote. Adams' support was thus crucial in allowing President Washington to remove appointees without the Senate's consent, in the commercial reprisal on Great Britain, on financial matters, in the location of the nation's capital and with the policy of neutrality.

Adams was re-elected as Vice President in 1792, by receiving 77 Electoral College votes. He cast the deciding vote that defeated the Republicans attempt to waylay John Jay's mission to England to procure a treaty. He also cast the deciding vote against suspending all trade with Britain.

In the presidential election of 1796, John Adams won the office with 71 Electoral College votes.

The Term of John Adams

Events: 1797

<u>March 1797</u>

- In his Inaugural Address President John Adams spoke about the history of the country and how events had progressed from the Revolutionary War days to the present government under the Constitution. He noted his contributions as Commissioner and Minister to the creation of the government, and he spoke of his veneration for the Constitution. He cited his own three-vote margin of victory as a sign to be vigilant for any corruption in future elections that could be decided by a single vote. He commended George Washington for leading the country for eight years, and he hoped that Washington's successors would use him as an example in the conduction of the affairs of state. He set forth his beliefs and guiding principles, and he concluded his address by stating his intent to support the Constitution of the United States.
- John Adams retained Washington's cabinet which was as follows:
  - Timothy Pickering as Secretary of State. In 1800, President Adams dismissed Secretary of State Timothy Pickering. President Adams then appointed John Marshall as Secretary of State.
  - Oliver Wolcott as Secretary of the Treasury
  - James McHenry as Secretary of War. In 1800, Secretary of War James McHenry was asked to resign by President Adams. President Adams then appointed Samuel Dexter as the Secretary of War
  - Joseph Habersham as Postmaster General
  - Charles Lee as Attorney General.
  - In 1798, when Congress created the position, Benjamin Stoddert was named by President Adams to be the new Secretary of the Navy.

<u>May 1797</u>

- John Adams addressed Congress to inform them of the crisis situation with France. President Adams wanted to maintain a peace with France—especially since the United States army consisted of only 3,500 men.

<u>June 1797</u>

- Congress passed a bill authorizing an 80,000-man militia in case a war should break out with France.

<u>July 1797</u>

- Congress approved an act to provide for Naval armament to equip and man 3 frigates: the *Constitution*, the *United States* and the *Constellation*.

- The House considered duties on stamps and passed a bill limiting the act for 5 years.

<u>August 1797</u>

- The United States signed a treaty with Tunis and agreed to pay a higher tribute in order to stop the attacks of the Barbary Pirates on American shipping.

<u>October 1797</u>

- The peace commission arrived at Paris, France to negotiate a treaty.

<u>November 1797</u>

- John Adams addressed the Congress and stated that a mercantile marine and a military marine were both necessary for the protection of the flourishing American commerce.

Events: 1798

<u>January 1798</u>

- The Eleventh Amendment to the Constitution was ratified by the states. This amendment forbids suits against a state by a citizen of another state—or that of a foreign nation.

<u>March 1798</u>

- President John Adams informed the Congress that the negotiations with France had failed. The Senate requested that President Adams provide all of the communications given to and received from the peace Commissioners at Paris, France.

<u>April 1798</u>

- Congress created the Mississippi Territory.
- The House requested that President Adams turn over the text of all dispatches concerning the peace negotiations. President Adams sent all dispatches concerning the negotiations to the House.

<u>May 1798</u>

- Congress created the Department of the Navy. It also authorized the President to order the seizure of any armed French ships by American warships if they were found to be interfering with American shipping.

June 1798

- Congress passed a bill that abolished the system of imprisonment of debtors. It also passed a bill that suspended all commerce with France.
- Congress passed the Naturalization Act that extended the residency requirement in America for aliens to 14 years before they became eligible for United States citizenship.
- Congress passed the first and second Alien Acts that allowed the President to deport any alien deemed as dangerous to the United States.

July 1798

- Congress passed a direct tax on property, houses and slaves.
- Congress passed the third Enemy Aliens Act to permit the arrest, imprisonment and deportation of any alien of an enemy power.
- Congress repealed the treaties with France that had been made in 1788.
- Congress created the United States Marine Corps. This Marine battalion was to be separate from the Military Establishment and was to be deployed on armed vessels of the United States.
- Congress created the Marine Hospital Service, a precursor of the United States Public Health Service.
- Congress passed The Sedition Act that declared any anti-government activity to be a high misdemeanor punishable by a fine and imprisonment. The activities that were covered included the publication of any false, scandalous or malicious writing.

November 1798

- Kentucky adopted a set of resolutions in protest against the usurpation of power by the federal government, in particular against the Alien and Sedition Acts. A second set of resolutions was endorsed by Kentucky to protest the unconstitutionality of the actions by the federal government.
- 2 American ships were captured: the *Baltimore* by the British, and the *Retaliation* by the French.

December 1798

- Virginia adopted a set of resolutions in protest against the unconstitutional actions of power by the federal government.
- President Adams addressed the Congress about the situation with France. His intention was that America's desire for peace be the guiding principle.

Events: 1799

January 1799

- Congress passed the Logan Act that made it illegal for any United States private citizen to conduct diplomatic negotiations with any foreign government.

February 1799

- The *Constitution* captured a French frigate, *L'Insurgente*.
- Congress passed the first quarantine act to enforce quarantine regulations in municipalities.
- The Senate approved a bill vesting the power of retaliation to the President. The bill was also extended to allow the President the use of the militia to execute the laws of the Union, suppress insurrections and repel foreign invasions.

March 1799

- President Adams issued a proclamation to call the disturbers of the peace in the Fries Rebellion to disperse and go back to their homes.

May 1799

- John Adams issued a proclamation that pardoned all of the participants of the Fries Rebellion.

December 1799

- The President addressed the Congress and mentioned the status of relations between the United States and that of France and England.
- The House resolved to work on amending the judiciary system, on the expenditure of public moneys, and in bolstering the national defense.
- The House also called for a new census of the inhabitants of the United States.

Events: 1800

January 1800

- The Senate considered the question of amending the Constitution with regard to the election of the President and Vice President.

February 1800

- The *Constellation* engaged in a naval battle with the French vessel *La Vengeance*.

March 1800

- The House proposed a bill for the establishment of a military academy, and for organizing the Corps of Engineers.
- The Senate worked on a bill to amend the judicial courts.

- The Senate addressed the issue of how to deal with disputed elections for the President and Vice President of the United States.

April 1800

- Congress passed the first Federal Bankruptcy Act although it only applied to merchants and traders.
- Congress established the Library of Congress, and President Adams approved the purchase of books for the new Library of Congress with $5,000 that had been appropriated by Congress.
- The House made appropriations for the military for $3,000,000, and considered the establishment of a military academy. It also proposed a bill for the appointment of one Vice Admiral and 4 Rear Admirals in the Navy.

May 1800

- Congress divided the existing Northwest Territory into the Indiana Territory and the Ohio Territory, and began offering 320-acre tracts for sale.

June 1800

- John Adams moved into Washington, D.C., the new capital city of the United States.

September 1800

- The second United States census recorded a population of over 5,300,000 inhabitants.

November 1800

- President Adams became the first to occupy the President's House.
- President Adams delivered his last address to the Congress, and spoke about relations with France, recommended further measures for a defensive naval force, and talked about the need for amending the judiciary system.

Events: 1801

February 1801

- In the presidential election, Thomas Jefferson and Aaron Burr wound up in a tie with 73 votes each. Since a tie resulted, the election was referred to the House of Representatives for resolution. The House finally decided on the 36th ballot taken. Thomas Jefferson was elected President and Aaron Burr became Vice President.

- Congress passed the Judiciary Act that reduced the number of Supreme Court Justices to 5, created a total of 16 circuit courts and added 23 new judges.

<u>March 1801</u>

- Thomas Jefferson took the oath of office of President as administered by Chief Justice John Marshall.

Later Years

Adams retired to his farm, and spent most of his time reading or cultivating. In 1818, his wife Abigail died. In 1820, he was chosen to be a delegate to the Massachusetts State convention to revise the state constitution. John Adams died at the age of 91 at Quincy, Massachusetts on July 4, 1826

Legacy

John Adams' greatest contribution was in keeping the United States from getting involved in a war with either France or England. The enhancement of the navy was his most outstanding achievement. Adams recognized that a superior navy was preferable to having a large army because marine forces would be better able to defend the coastlines, to protect American shipping, and fight a defensive war with either France or England. Under his administration the number of ships increased to 50 and the number of officers and seamen increased to 5,000. By making peace with France, Adams set the stage for the Louisiana Purchase in 1803 by President Thomas Jefferson.

Adams shaped the fate of American history by his decisive actions as a Congressman, diplomat and President. He also influenced the evolution of the Judiciary by his appointment of John Marshall as Chief Justice of the Supreme Court. Adams was a visionary who foresaw many of the immediate events as well as futuristic social outcomes. In 1755, Adams predicted that the growing population of North America would surpass that of England—and that the seat of world power would be transferred from England to America via some development. Adams also predicted that the United States would one day be the greatest empire in the world. In 1819, he envisioned that the conflict over slavery would be the most important problem facing the country, and that it would have the potential to divide the union and produce a conflict with violence and bloodshed. Ultimately, he believed that the abolition of slavery would be achieved, that the status for women would be improved, and that the country would grow in population to more than 200,000,000 inhabitants.

Thomas Jefferson

The Third President Under the Constitution

Early Years

Thomas Jefferson was born in Albemarle County, Virginia on April 13, 1743. His father was Peter Jefferson, and his mother was Jane Randolph. Taught by his father to read and write, Jefferson read all of his father's books by the age of 5. Jefferson's early schooling was at a nearby private school in Tuckahoe where he learned classical languages and mathematics. Jefferson also taught himself music and became a violinist.

When his father died in 1757, Jefferson inherited one-half of a 7500-acre estate and 60 slaves—although the will stated that he would not own these until he turned 21. Jefferson continued his studies at another private school at Edgeworth where the curriculum included the study of Greek, Latin and French languages and natural philosophy. Jefferson read the original works of Homer, Plato, Virgil, Ovid, Livy, Cicero and Horace in addition to the French literature of the Enlightenment era. Jefferson also read the works of Shakespeare, Chaucer, Butler, Milton, Pope, Horace and Mallet.

Jefferson entered William and Mary College in 1760, where he studied law, literature, philosophy, science and mathematics. Jefferson became acquainted with the works of Montesquieu, Moliere, Voltaire, Rousseau, Locke, Hume and Diderot. He graduated in 1762, and then studied law for the next 5 years. During this time he was immersed in the works of Blackstone, Coke, Bacon, Gilbert and Fonblanque, and he also pursued his studies of classical writers such as Condorcet, Hutcheson and Lord Kame.

In 1762, Jefferson was elected surveyor of Albemarle County, Virginia. In 1764, he was elected as Justice of the Peace. In 1764, he also assumed the estate that his father had willed to him. In 1766, he was greatly influenced by the five-volume work entitled *Philosophical Transactions* by Viscount Henry Saint-John Bolingbroke. He adopted Bolingbroke's philosophical views that included materialism, the rejection of metaphysics and religion, and a belief in reason as the sole arbiter of knowledge and worth.

After he was admitted to the bar in 1767, Jefferson practiced law in Williamsburg, Virginia. His earnings from his law practice dealing with land patents with over 500 cases on his books in one year allowed him to begin construction of his home at Monticello in 1768. In 1772, he married Martha Wayles Skelton. When Martha's father died, Jefferson added to his personal inheritance an amount of 5,000 acres and 135 additional slaves. Thus, Jefferson became one of the greatest landholders in Virginia. In June 1774, he turned his law business over to his cousin, Edmund Randolph.

The Virginia Legislature

Jefferson served in the Virginia House of Burgesses in 1769. He voted to approve the Virginia Resolves that delineated the rights of colonists. Governor Norborne Berkeley Botetourt dissolved the Assembly in 1769, and Jefferson joined others at the Raleigh Tavern to adopt an Association agreement. The agreement barred the importation or consumption of British goods, and was signed by 94 of the 115 participants. In 1770, another agreement was created for a stronger nonimportation statement and boycott which Jefferson and 100 others signed.

Jefferson did not return to the Virginia Assembly until 1773, at which time he participated in the creation of the Committee of Correspondence. When Governor Dunmore dissolved the Virginia Legislature in 1774, Jefferson met once again with a group of 100 others at the Raleigh Tavern. There they formulated a plan to oppose British taxation without representation.

The House of Burgesses was restored again in 1774. However, Virginia Governor Dunmore dissolved it again. Once more Jefferson met at the Raleigh Tavern with a group that proposed the formation of the First Continental Congress. Jefferson was not able to attend, but he did write a paper entitled *A Summary View of the Rights of British America*. It was a declaration that Americans had the right to govern themselves. Thereafter, Jefferson devoted most of his time producing a draft of a new Constitution for Virginia. He included a provision for religious freedom, and that the constitution should be ratified by a special convention—rather than by the sitting legislature.

Delegate to the Second Continental Congress: 1775-1776

Jefferson attended the Second Continental Congress in 1775. Jefferson wrote the draft for the *Declaration on Taking up Arms*—a document that declared that the English Parliament had no right to exercise authority over the colonies. This document was delivered to the British as a petition that asked for relief by the King.

Jefferson attended the Second Continental Congress in 1776. Jefferson was appointed to the committee that was tasked with writing the Declaration of Independence. Jefferson was assigned the task of writing the declaration, and he submitted the first draft to the Congress in June 1776. This document laid the foundation of human equality and freedom for the new nation.

Jefferson took notes on the debates concerning the proposed Articles of Confederation. As a member of the committee tasked with the assignment, he presented his ideas for the design of the Great Seal of the United States. Jefferson was also chosen to be on a committee charged with drawing up the rules and regulations for the conduct of the Congress during debates. And, he was on a committee that dealt with regulating the post office. With regard to the currency of the United States, he was in favor of it being based on the Spanish milled dollar system with decimal notation to reflect parts of a dollar.

In 1776, Jefferson left the Second Continental Congress to return to his Monticello home in Virginia. In September 1776, Jefferson was elected as a Commissioner to the court of France but declined to go.

Revolutionary Leader of Virginia

In 1776, Jefferson returned to the Virginia House of Delegates. He submitted 126 different bills to the Virginia Legislature that embodied the new democracy principles— many of which became the guiding principles for the federal government of the United States. Among these were the establishment of religious freedom, a more enlightened penal code system, and a push for free public education.

In 1779, Jefferson was elected by the Virginia Legislature as Governor. His administration was beset by problems of widespread tax resistance, by ineffective attempts to seize the estates of Loyalists, by failures to obtain money through loans, and by depreciation of the currency. He was the Governor when the British attacked the Chesapeake Bay area with 60 ships and 5,000 troops in 1780. British General Benedict Arnold ordered 1,600 troops in a personal quest to dismantle the government of Virginia at Richmond, including the capture of Governor Jefferson. Jefferson fled, but the British troops ransacked his quarters, and burned about three-fourths of his personal papers and library. Jefferson fled to his home, the British troops attacked Virginia again and the British went after Jefferson, the Virginia Council and the General Assembly. Jefferson narrowly escaped being captured at his mansion.

In 1781, Jefferson retired as Governor of Virginia and returned to private life. He declined to accept the appointment as a Minister to France. In 1782, his wife Martha died. In 1782, he again received an appointment as minister to France to work on the treaty between American and England. This time he accepted, but through a series of circumstances he was not able to go to France. In 1783, the Virginia Legislature again chose him as a delegate to the Second Continental Congress.

Delegate to the Second Continental Congress: 1783-1784

Jefferson attended the Second Continental Congress in 1783. He reviewed the peace treaty with England, and was on a committee to devise a plan for the temporary government of the western territory. He wrote some of the language for treaties of amity and commerce that were to be formed with other countries. He also suggested that treaties be done with Morocco, Algiers, Tunis and Tripoli. And, he helped in the adoption of the decimal system of coinage for American money.

In 1784, Jefferson helped to create an act under which temporary and permanent governments could be established in the western territory. He also participated in writing the conditions under which a new state could be admitted to the union. This legislation served as the foundation for the Northwest Ordinance that was passed in 1787 to govern the Northwest Territory.

Jefferson was on a committee that recommended that each state send delegates to the Congress for a period of one year. In addition, he worked on the reform of the coin system, and he successfully urged that the American dollar be based on decimal units. However, he was unsuccessful in trying to replace the English system of weights and measures with metric standards.

Foreign Minister to France

Jefferson was elected as Minister to France in 1784. He sailed aboard the merchant ship *Ceres* and arrived in Paris, France. He saw the start of the French Revolution, and the atrocities that he witnessed provided him with a valuable lesson that taught him the consequences of bad government and social inequality. In 1786, Jefferson was able to obtain a treaty with Morocco to achieve a truce with the Barbary pirates.

Secretary of State

Jefferson sailed aboard the *Clermont* from France and returned to Norfolk, Virginia in 1789. He accepted President George Washington's offer to be Secretary of State in 1790. In this position he laid the foundation of rules and regulations for conducting the diplomatic affairs of the United States, including political rights, neutrality, peace, trade and friendship. Jefferson recommended to President Washington that he close the American mission in London, which President Washington did as suggested.

Jefferson opposed the establishment of a United States Bank. In 1790, Jefferson forged a deal with Alexander Hamilton to have the national capital be located by the Potomac River in return for Jefferson's backing of the proposal to have the government assume all outstanding state debts.

At the height of the French revolution in 1793, Jefferson urged a policy of neutrality. Jefferson submitted his resignation in July 1793, but President Washington persuaded him to remain in office until the December 1793. In December 1793, Jefferson retired from politics and remained at Monticello for the next 3 years.

Vice President

In the Electoral College Presidential result of 1797, Jefferson received 68 votes compared to John Adams who got 71 votes. Jefferson thus became the Vice President and emerged as a leader of the opposition political party. As the leader of the Senate, Jefferson devised the rules of procedure and wrote the parliamentary handbook for the Senate that is still in use today.

His opposition to the federal policies created a rift between him and President John Adams, especially with regard to the Alien and Sedition Acts of 1798. In response to the Alien and Sedition Acts, Jefferson collaborated with others to draft a manifesto of states' rights called the Kentucky Resolutions of 1798. These resolutions were followed by the

Virginia resolutions of 1798. The resolutions affirmed that the states were not in agreement on the submission of un-delegated powers to the federal government.

Presidential Election of 1800

Jefferson launched his presidential campaign in 1799. In 1801, Jefferson and Aaron Burr each received 73 Electoral College votes for President. The election was thrown into the House of Representatives, which after 36 ballots finally elected Jefferson to be President. In March 1801, Jefferson was inaugurated as the third Constitutional President—and the first to be inaugurated at the permanent capital in Washington, DC. Supreme Court Chief Justice John Marshall administered the oath to President Thomas Jefferson after he had delivered his Inaugural Address. With this election, President Jefferson gave birth to the beginning of a two-party system in the United States—something that has stood firm for over 215 years.

The First Term of Thomas Jefferson

Events: 1801

<u>March 1801</u>

- In his Inaugural Address Jefferson expressed his gratitude for having been elected, and asked the people to deal with one another with harmony and affection. He also wanted them to create a wise and frugal government. He sought peace, commerce and friendship with other nations—but with no entangling alliances in accordance with former President Washington's wishes. He stated his objectives in his commitment to states' rights, the dismantling of a standing army and navy, and the promotion of agriculture as the basis of trade surpluses. Above all he wanted to promote the freedom of the press, the freedom of religion, the protection under habeas corpus, and the trial by juries that were impartially selected. He reminded the audience that the minority had equal rights that were to be protected under the equality of the law to guard against oppression.
- President Jefferson's cabinet was comprised as follows:
    - James Madison as Secretary of State
    - Samuel Dexter as Secretary of the Treasury. In May 1801, President Jefferson appointed Albert Gallatin as the Secretary of the Treasury.
    - Henry Dearborn as Secretary of War
    - Robert Smith as Secretary of the Navy. In April 1801, Benjamin Stoddert became the new Secretary of the Navy.
    - Joseph Habersham as Postmaster General. In November 1801, Gideon Granger was appointed by President Jefferson as Postmaster General.
    - Levi Lincoln as Attorney General.
- When President Jefferson assumed office, the debt of the United States stood at $83,000,000.
- President Jefferson established the principle of the Chief Executive acting as Judge by pardoning and freeing persons who had been jailed under the Sedition Acts of 1798.

<u>May 1801</u>

President Jefferson sent 3 frigates and a sloop of war to battle against Barbary pirates that were operating off the North African coast in the Mediterranean Sea. These Muslim pirates had exacted $18,000 in tribute from America in 1799 to guarantee safe passage for United States ships from several European states. When Pasha declared war on America, Jefferson sent a naval squadron to the Mediterranean Sea to form a blockade of Tripoli. In 1801, the *Enterprise* seized the corsair *Tripoli* as part of this enforcement. This became the first foreign military adventure by the United States.

- President Jefferson delivered his written address to Congress in which he cited the lessening of hostilities with foreign powers. The only exception that Jefferson noted was the conflict with the Barbary States, especially with Tripoli. He cited the census of 1800 that projected an increase in numbers such that the population would double in 22 years. He also mentioned the problems of revenue, the need for reduction of expenditures, and the issue of keeping a standing military force in case of attack.
- The House agreed that it was expedient that the President be authorized to protect the commerce of the United States against the Barbary pirates.
- The House appropriated $1,000 for one year to spend on the Library of Congress. An unexpended balance of $2,800 that had previously been appropriated was also to be used for the purchase of books.

Events: 1802

January 1802

- President Jefferson requested that Congress repeal the Judiciary Act of 1801.
- Jefferson gave his position regarding the separation of church and state. He stated that by means of the First Amendment a wall of separation had been built.
- The House considered a bill concerning fugitives from justice.
- The Senate approved the bill from the House for reapportionment that the House had set at a ratio of 33,000 to 1.

February 1802

- Congress authorized the arming of merchant ships to protect themselves against Tripoli. Although Congress did not declare war, it did authorize the use of force at sea.

March 1802

- President Jefferson signed the repeal of the Judiciary Act of 1801 that had been passed by the Congress.
- Congress established the United States Military Academy at West Point, New York, which opened in 1802.

April 1802

- Congress abolished the whisky tax and all other excise duties.
- Congress nullified the Naturalization Act of 1798. In its place Congress reinstated the original Naturalization Act of 1795 that required only 5 years of residency for an alien to be eligible for citizenship.

- Congress passed a new Judiciary Act setting the number of Supreme Court Justices to 6, and the number of circuit courts to 6.
- Congress passed the Enabling Act that permitted any territory organized under the Ordinance of 1787 to become a state.
- The Senate began discussions on the redemption of the public debt with recommendations by Secretary of the Treasury Gallatin to allocate an amount equal to $7,300,000 on a yearly basis for a period of 16 years to pay it off.

May 1802

- Washington, D.C. was incorporated as a city by Congress.

August 1802

- President Jefferson sent the *John Adams* to the Mediterranean Sea to fortify the American Navy forces against the Barbary pirates.

December 1802

- President Jefferson addressed the Congress in which he praised the peace and friendship abroad, and the law and order at home. He cited the British for their continuing practice of impressment of United States sailors, and the conflict with the Barbary pirates of the Mediterranean.

Events: 1803

January 1803

- President Jefferson appointed James Monroe as a minister to France to negotiate with Robert R. Livingston for the purpose of purchasing New Orleans and West Florida from the French. He instructed Charles Pinckney, the American minister to Spain, to become involved in the discussions. He also requested funds from Congress—an appropriation of $2,500—for an expedition to be led by Meriwether Lewis and William Clark that would reach to the Pacific Ocean.
- The House recommended the adoption of a resolution that appropriated $2,000,000 to defray expenses incurred between the United States and foreign nations. This money was actually appropriated to assist the United States as a sum towards the purchase of Louisiana.

February 1803

- Ohio became the seventeenth state to enter the Union.
- John Marshall, with his ruling in *Marbury vs. Madison,* established the principle of judicial review of federal legislation and executive action. Chief Justice Marshall increased the balance of power among the 3 branches of the Federal Government by declaring an act of Congress unconstitutional.

- The Senate authorized a force of 80,000 militia for use by the President.

- The American envoys Monroe and Livingston acquired the Louisiana Purchase from France for $15,000,000. The agreement added a territory of 1,000,000 square miles that more than doubled the size of the United States and made it into one of the largest nations. The action also enhanced the implied powers of the President that were not specifically granted by the Constitution.
- In the undeclared war against Tripoli, President Jefferson appointed Edward Preble as Commander of the Mediterranean Naval Squadron.

September 1803

- President Jefferson sent Meriwether Lewis and William Clark on an expedition to the Pacific Coast, a journey that was intended to be one of exploration and discovery.

October 1803

- The President addressed the Congress and asked the Senate to ratify the treaty for the purchase of the Louisiana Territory. He also asked the House to authorize the issuance of bonds to pay for the purchase.
- The *Philadelphia* was captured by the Tripoli pirates.
- The Senate approved the treaty for the Louisiana Purchase.

November 1803

- The House approved the funding for the Louisiana Purchase, and appropriated $11,250,000 in bonds for its acquisition.

December 1803

- Congress passed the Twelfth Amendment to the Constitution to provide for separate ballots in voting for the offices of President and Vice President.

Events: 1804

February 1804

- In the undeclared war against Tripoli, the *Intrepid* won a battle in which the *Philadelphia*, was recaptured, with its American crew killing the Muslim crew in hand-to-hand combat.

March 1804

- Congress passed the Land Act setting the price of public lands at $1.64 per acre for 164-acre tracts. Congress also split the Louisiana Territory into two parts: the Territory of Orleans and the District of Louisiana.

April 1804

- In the undeclared war against Tripoli, two more vessels were captured from the Tripoli pirates.

July 1804

- Vice President Aaron Burr fatally shot Alexander Hamilton in a duel.

August 1804

- American Commodore Preble bombarded the city of Tripoli in a series of 5 attacks with his warship.

September 1804

- The Twelfth Amendment to the Constitution was ratified by the states.

November 1804

- President Jefferson addressed the Congress on the subjects of the Louisiana Purchase and the battle against the Barbary pirates.

December 1804

- Thomas Jefferson was reelected to a second term by an Electoral vote of 162.
- A bill to divide the Indiana Territory into 2 separate governments was passed by the Senate.

Events: 1805

January 1805

- The Michigan Territory was formed by dividing the Indiana Territory.

March 1805

- Congress affirmed the purchase of the Louisiana Territory by enacting legislation to confirm the land grants from both France and Spain. It also transformed the Louisiana District back into the Louisiana Territory, and granted self-government and a representative assembly.

The Second Term of Thomas Jefferson

Events: 1805

<u>March 1805</u>

- In his Inaugural Address, Jefferson vowed to discontinue internal taxes and instead shift the burden to consumption taxes based on imported luxury items. He wanted support for a federally financed public works program, and proposed a "pay-as-you-go" system of fiscal policy. He briefly touched on the acquisition of the Louisiana Territory noting that the enlargement of the country would present some danger to the Union. With respect to religion, he again mentioned the importance of separation of church and state. Finally, he expressed his support for the freedom of the press.
- The President's cabinet was as follows:
  - Secretary of State James Madison
  - Secretary of the Treasury Albert Gallatin
  - Secretary of War Henry Dearborn
  - Secretary of the Navy Jacob Crowinshield
  - Attorney General Robert Smith
  - Postmaster General Gideon Granger.

<u>April 1805</u>

- A combination of 100 Turkish and Greek mercenaries, and 8 American Marines captured the port of Derna, Tripoli in a victory assisted by a bombardment from United States ships on Derna.

<u>June 1805</u>

- A peace treaty was signed between the United States and Tripoli. Tripoli granted the American Navy the right to sail the Mediterranean Sea. In return, the United States agreed to pay a one-time ransom of $60,000 for the release of the American crew of the *Philadelphia*.

<u>December 1805</u>

- The President addressed the Congress and noted that the nations in Europe were in great turmoil. He was thankful for the resolution to the conflict with Tripoli, especially with the liberation of the American prisoners of war who had been captured by the Barbary pirates.
- The House considered appropriations to protect the ports and harbors, and to build gunboats and battleships.

Events: 1806

<u>January 1806</u>

- The House considered a bill for the establishment of rules for the armies of the United States, including the authorization of courts martial to punish incidents of mutiny and sedition. It also organized and classified the militia into four classes, and it excluded minors from the service.
- The Senate considered a bill for classification of the militia—the initial precursor of the draft—and made all men between the ages of 18 to 45 eligible for land service. The only allowances for exemptions were those that were based on religious beliefs. Otherwise, any person who refused duty if drafted would be arrested as a deserter.

February 1806

- President Jefferson signed a bill passed by Congress allocating $2,000,000 for the purchase of Florida from Spain. However, Emperor Napoleon of France decided that it should remain in Spanish hands and the bill was for naught.

March 1806

- An accounting of the militia showed it to be about ten percent of the United States population—a population that was estimated to be 6,000,000 persons.
- Congress authorized the building of the Cumberland Road from Maryland to Virginia.
- The House passed a bill that prohibited the plurality of government office holding by Army and Navy officers of the United States.

April 1806

- Congress passed the Nicholson Act—a law that forbade the importation of an enumerated list of items from England.

May 1806

- The British ship *Leander* fired a shot off Sandy Hook by New York that killed a man in another ship. President Jefferson issued a proclamation charging the Captain of the *Leander* with murder, and ordered the *Leander* and two other vessels out of American waters.

July 1806

- The trials of Samuel Ogden and William S. Smith who were involved with the *Leander* resulted in acquittals for both of them.

November 1806

- President Jefferson issued a proclamation warning American citizens from becoming involved in any illegal expedition against the Spanish.

<u>December 1806</u>

- President Jefferson addressed the Congress, and mentioned the difficulties with Spain over the Florida territory. He also referred to the peace arrangements with the Barbary pirates, and to the expeditions of Lewis and Clark, and that of Pike.

Events: 1807

<u>January 1807</u>

- Tunis accepted $10,000 for a Tunisian ship that had been seized by Commodore Rodgers.
- Luther Baldwin was indicted for sedition for making demeaning and malicious statements against President Jefferson.
- The House resolved that the prosecution of a person at common law for libel was a violation of the freedom of the press, and contrary to the Constitution of the United States. It further resolved that in all prosecutions, whether criminal or otherwise, it was the natural right of the citizen to give in evidence the truth.

<u>February 1807</u>

- The House considered a motion to make further provisions to secure the writ of *habeas corpus* for persons in custody under the authority of the United States.

<u>March 1807</u>

- Congress passed a law making the slave trade illegal starting in January 1808.
- Aaron Burr was charged with treason in a federal district court at Richmond, Virginia.

<u>June 1807</u>

- The British frigate *Leopard* opened fire on the American frigate *Chesapeake* off the coast of Norfolk, Virginia. 3 Americans were killed, 18 were wounded, and 4 were taken as prisoners for allegedly being British deserters. As a result, President Jefferson issued a proclamation for all British ships to leave the territorial waters of the United States.
- Aaron Burr was indicted for treason, and his trial date was set for August 1807, in the Richmond, Virginia federal court.

<u>September 1807</u>

- The Aaron Burr trial was presided over by United States Supreme Court Chief Justice John Marshall. Burr was acquitted of treason charges.

October 1807

- In his message to the Congress, President Jefferson proclaimed his love of peace, but he also indicated that the events concerning the British would require having a larger militia to deal with these threats.

November 1807

- The Senate passed a resolution requesting President Jefferson to have the British account for the names and status of all American seamen who had been impressed into the Royal Navy.

December 1807

- Congress passed the first Embargo Act as requested by President Jefferson who cited the increasing dangers to American shipping. The law forbade any American products to be exported and also forbade any American ships to set sail for foreign ports.
- Congress authorized the construction of 188 gunboats by allocating $852,000.

Events: 1808

January 1808

- Congress passed a second Embargo Act that forbade the exportation of any goods by either sea or land.

February 1808

- President Jefferson asked for an increase of 6,000 men to the United States Army.
- The Senate considered a bill to punish treason and other crimes and offenses against the United States.

March 1808

- Congress passed a Third Embargo Act that closed off all overland and waterborne trade in the United States.
- The House considered a bill to punish conspiracies and acts of treason.
- The House considered a bill to establish a system of military courts.

April 1808

- President Jefferson transmitted to the Senate a report on roads and canals that represented the most comprehensive and constructive domestic program.
- Congress passed an act that authorized the President to suspend the embargo.

- Congress passed an act that authorized the enforcement of the new embargo against France and England.
- The House voted to approve of a bill to increase the army and on a resolution to appropriate $1,000,000 for the new forces. The House also considered an appropriation of $200,000 to assist the states in increasing the size of their combined militias by 100,000 men.

November 1808

President Jefferson addressed the Congress and talked about the belligerent situation with both England and France. He also talked about being at peace with the Barbary pirates. And, he spoke about having reduced the national debt by almost $34,000,000.

December 1808

- James Madison won the election for President with 122 Electoral College votes.

Events: 1809

January 1809

- Congress passed the Enforcement Act to halt smuggling activities.
- The House considered increasing the military force in the United States as a preparation in case of war.

February 1809

- Chief Justice John Marshall strengthened the power of the national government over that of state governments in his decision in the case of *United States v. Peters*. His ruling concerning the nullification of a federal court order by Pennsylvania was used against all states that were trying to rescind the Embargo Acts.

March 1809

- Congress passed the Non-Intercourse Act, a law that repealed the Embargo Acts that had caused a severe economic depression. The new act permitted trade with any country except France and England.
- James Madison was inaugurated as the Fourth President of the United States, being sworn in by Chief Justice John Marshall.

Later Years

Thomas Jefferson retired to Monticello, Virginia, ending a political career that spanned over 44 years. In 1823, Jefferson answered a letter to give advice to President James Monroe on the issue of keeping European powers out of the Americas—a reply that became the Monroe Doctrine. This declaration stated that any attempt by Europeans to colonize the Americas or to interfere in the internal affairs of the Western Hemisphere would be considered as dangerous to the peace and security of the United States.

In 1817, Jefferson started working on an educational system for Virginia since he believed that education was the only hope in changing attitudes, in improving morality and in spreading civilization. In 1825, the University of Virginia began its curriculum, with its guiding purpose being to provide for the diffusion of knowledge among the people of Virginia. Confronted by poverty due to debts, he sold his 6,860-book library collection to the United States Government in 1814 for $24,076. His private library became the new beginning of the Library of Congress that had been burned by the British in the War of 1812.

In 1826, Jefferson suffered a severe attack of diarrhea—a malady that led to his health deteriorating significantly. On July 4, 1826, Thomas Jefferson died at the age of 83, leaving behind a huge debt of $107,000 and 170 slaves who were subsequently sold at auction.

Legacy

Jefferson's most crowning achievement was the acquisition of the Louisiana Territory in 1803. In the process he broadened the interpretation of the Constitution instead of waiting for an Amendment to authorize such a purchase. He also sponsored the explorations of Lewis and Clark into the Northwest, and the Pikes expedition into the Southwest. He was very active in the reduction of tax burdens, in cutting spending and following a course of government frugality, for he was intent on having a very minimum public debt for the United States. The most significant legal event was the signing into law of the act that forbade any further importation of slaves into the United States starting in 1808. In his actions he attempted to be the guardian of democratic rights for the individual, for local governments and for state governments. This was especially true in the area of personal belief in which he maintained that government—in accordance with the Constitution— had nothing to do with religion.

In foreign affairs he was successful in defeating the threat of the Barbary pirates, and he was able to ensure American shipping from being subjected to further attacks by Muslim countries. He also averted a potentially damaging diplomatic situation by arresting Aaron Burr and charging him with treason in federal court. Even though Burr was acquitted, he was prevented from carrying out his land conspiracy scheme of forcibly acquiring Mexico from Spain. Finally, although the trade embargoes that he decreed pushed the country into the worst depression since the Revolutionary War, his actions served to avert a full-scale war with England—and possibly with France.

James Madison

The Fourth President Under the Constitution

Early Years

James Madison was born in King George County, Virginia on March 16, 1751. His father was James Madison Sr. who was a plantation owner, and his mother was Nelly Conway Madison. His first schooling covered the fundamentals of reading, writing and arithmetic. In 1762, he enrolled in the Robertson school where he studied Latin, Greek, French, Spanish and Italian languages, mathematics, geography, logic and literature. After spending 5 years at the Robertson school, Madison left in 1767, to study at home.

In 1769, Madison enrolled at the College of New Jersey at Princeton. He mastered English, Latin and Greek and he studied science, geography, logic, rhetoric, mathematics and natural philosophy. He also acquired a foundation based on the lore, history and wisdom of the ancient Greek and Roman civilizations. In 1771, Madison graduated from Princeton. However, he injured his health by studying to excess—almost to the exclusion of sleep. He had frequent bouts of illness, and in 1772, he went to Berkeley warm springs near Winchester, Virginia to restore his health.

Virginia Politics

In 1774, Madison was elected to the Orange County Committee that was charged with enforcing the resolves of the First Continental Congress. He also procured and distributed arms and supplies. In 1775, he was commissioned as a Colonel in the Orange County militia. However, he never took part in the Revolutionary War since his bad health and liability to sudden attacks prevented him from participation in the army.

In 1776, Madison was elected to serve in the Virginia Convention. The task of the convention was to act on resolves by the voters and to send instructions to the Representatives from Virginia who were attending the Second Continental Congress in Philadelphia. The convention also approved of the resolution for independence that had been created by the Second Continental Congress. Madison was on another committee that prepared a Declaration of Rights and a plan of government to maintain peace and order in the colony. In 1777, Madison was elected to the Virginia House of Delegates. He was then elected to the Council on which he served until 1779.

Second Continental Congress: 1780-1783

Madison attended the Second Continental Congress as a delegate in March 1780 where he was a member of the Board of Admiralty. In 1781, he was assigned to a committee whose job was to announce the Articles of Confederation to the public. He was appointed to a committee that was responsible for preparing a plan for the execution of all acts and resolutions passed within the Articles of Confederation. And, he was on a committee concerned with creating an ordinance for collecting the duty on imports and prizes.

In 1782, Madison was on a committee that was responsible for devising ways and means to prevent illicit trade with the enemy. In 1783, he was on a committee tasked with considering the means of restoring public credit and of obtaining from the states substantial funds for funding the entire debt of the United States. He was also on a committee whose responsibility was to determine what further steps were to be taken to carry out the articles of peace between the United States and Great Britain.

Return to Virginia

Madison left the Second Continental Congress in 1783 and returned to Virginia. He purchased 1,000 acres of land that he later sold at a 200 per cent profit. He served as a Representative in the Virginia Assembly from 1784 to 1786. In 1785, he adopted and help pass Thomas Jefferson's bill for establishing religious freedom.

Second Continental Congress: 1786-1788

Madison attended the Second Continental Congress as a delegate in 1786. In 1787, he was on a committee that was appointed to consider the condition of the military establishment of the United States. In 1788, he was on a committee that advised Congress on treating with Spain for the surrender of their claim to the navigation of the Mississippi River.

Constitutional Convention: 1787

Madison's frustration with the Articles of Confederation provided him with many lessons as to how to create a more effective government. When he attended the Annapolis Convention in September 1786, he readily agreed to the call for a Constitutional Convention to be held in Philadelphia, Pennsylvania in 1787. In Madison's view, the Articles of Confederation functioned merely as a treaty of friendship rather than as an effective government of law. When the Constitutional Convention began in 1787, Madison was among the delegates. He introduced his plan of government consisting of 15 resolutions, which was then presented to the convention as its basic working document.

In the first action by the delegates, Alexander Hamilton proposed that the convention create a new national government. The convention agreed to create a new constitution that established supreme legislative, executive and judiciary bodies. This was the first major test of the assumed power of the delegates who had only been tasked to modify the existing Articles of Confederation. The next debate centered on whether each state should have an equal vote in the legislature, or instead be represented on the basis of population. The compromise that was reached was that the lower house would be elected by the people. The convention then debated the composition, powers and the method of election for the executive. The delegates accepted only a very general definition of executive powers, but postponed other matters, including the method of election for the executive, although they did agree to have a single executive.

The issue of an executive veto was tempered by the resolution to include a provision for an override of an executive veto by a two-thirds majority vote by the legislature. The convention also decided to institute national courts as established by the national legislature, but deferred on the method of appointing the judges. Further debates established the length of time for a Representative to be that of 2 years only, and that the term for a Senator be fixed at 6 years. The convention also agreed to have equal representation in the Senate. Next, the convention approved of clauses making the national legislature and its acts be the supreme law to which the state courts and state legislatures would be subordinate. Then, the agreement was reached by which each state would have 2 Senators.

The debates continued over the issue of ratification of the Constitution. By agreement it was decided that the state legislatures would vote on it, and that this would be the best way of settling all disputes and doubts. Also established was that the provisions of the Constitution would be supreme, that the courts were to judge statue law by its conformity to the Constitution, and that no state had a right to nullify the law of the land.

The powers of the Congress were debated next, in particular, the provisions to create revenue, the taxing of imports, the establishing of post offices, the power to declare war and to govern the territories. Additional powers that were debated were those of granting patents and copyrights, establishing a university, and promoting useful arts and discoveries.

In September 1787, agreement was finally reached with respect to the executive powers, and on the method of choosing the executive. The President would be chosen by an Electoral College ballot, he would have a term of 4 years and be eligible for re-election. The executive would have the power to appoint judges, ambassadors and other officials—subject only to the consent of the Senate. The House of Representatives was given the power to choose the President in the event that the Electoral College failed to find a majority vote. The Senate was given the power to conduct impeachment trials— including those for the chief executive. The regulation of trade was agreed to, and the margin for a legislative override of an executive veto was reduced from three-fourths to only two-thirds.

In September 1787, the Constitution was engrossed and the convention adjourned with the only task left to do being the signing of the document. The ratio of inhabitants to a Representative within a state was changed from 40,000 to 1 to 30,000 to 1. Madison signed the Constitution in September 1787, as one of the 39 signers.

The Federalist Papers

Tench Coxe from Pennsylvania sent Madison some materials that were in support of the Constitution. Madison then consulted with John Jay and Alexander Hamilton in writing one of the most profound documents in American political history. Madison wrote 26 of the essays in the *Federalist Papers*, and he co-authored 3 more with Alexander Hamilton concerning the analysis of the Constitution and the political philosophy supporting it. Madison spoke on the advantages of having a well-constructed union, of the disadvantages of being in a confederacy, and on the sources of tyranny. He stated that the nature of the new government would result in frequent changes of those in power by the frequent elections. He argued that this situation would in turn produce frequent changes in the measures enacted into law.

Madison was in favor of the system of checks and balances for the proposed government because he knew that enlightened statesmen would not always be at the helm. He cited the fundamental foundation of the government as being based on the separate and distinct separation of the legislative, executive and judiciary branches. However, he made allowances for there being no barrier between any of these 3 separate powers so that dependencies and overlaps could exist in a harmonious manner.

In the *Federalist Papers* essays Madison attacked the existing Articles of Confederation because all of the power was vested in the legislative—the Continental Congress. In discussing where the powers of the new government were vested, and how these powers were distributed under the new proposed structure, Madison argued for the necessity of having these powers to promote the public good—including security. At the same time, he agreed that these powers would have to be safeguarded to prevent their perversion and misuse to the public detriment. He also cited the need for the power of taxation to provide for the common defense and general welfare.

As to the powers of government in regard to foreign issues, Madison pointed out the advantages in terms of dealing with foreign commerce, treaty making, the establishment of consuls, and the means to effectively counter acts of piracy and other felonies. And, in regard to the interstate relationships, he noted the advantages of the regulation of interstate commerce, and of the necessity of prohibition of the individual states coining their own money. He thought it important to have restraints on the states with regard to imports and exports, and he advocated the practicality of having a uniform standard of weights and measures. Madison also knew that it was essential that no state be allowed to enter into any treaties, alliances or confederations with foreign powers.

Of all the powers and provisions that were written into the Constitution, Madison held that the power to make all laws that are necessary to carry out the powers vested in the United States government was the most important of all. His contention was that this power was expressly given by the various sections of the Constitution. This was in contrast to the Articles of Confederation where the doctrine of construction or implication had to be applied to extend its powers to deal with changes in the future. It was this power that made the Constitution and the laws of the United States the supreme law of the land—with the ultimate authority residing in the people. Nevertheless, he stressed the preference of having a republic form of government rather than direct popular participation in the decisions of government.

Finally, Madison considered an unstable government to be one in which laws were made for the few rather than for the many. He saw that great injury would result to the economic sphere from a lack of confidence in the institutions of government if this instability were to be created. He also thought that responsibility should be limited to those objects that were within the power of the responsible group, and that this responsibility should relate to the operations of that power.

Virginia Ratification Convention

Madison returned to Virginia in 1788. Madison was enticed to support a bill of rights after the Constitution was ratified. Madison was elected as a delegate to serve in the Virginia ratification convention. He ordered a large supply of The *Federalist Papers* to hand out to the delegates of the convention. He attended the ratification convention in June 1788.

The ratification convention agreed to debate the Constitution on a clause-by-clause basis. This agreement provided Madison with a powerful advantage over the critics of the Constitution. A motion was made for approval of the Constitution, with a bill of rights to be added later. The delegates voted to ratify the Constitution, and to add amendments for later adoption as a bill of rights.

Return to Virginia Again

Madison returned to Virginia and was defeated in his quest for a seat in the Senate and for a seat in the House. However, Madison eventually became a Congressman from Virginia. In March 1789, Madison questioned the length and the content of the draft that Washington had composed for his Inaugural Address. Instead, Madison wrote a short and dignified speech that Washington delivered at his inauguration in April 1789. Madison also drafted Washington's replies to the House and the Senate.

Representative from Virginia: 1789-1797

As a Congressman, Madison moved that the Congress establish a revenue system to meet the debts and expenses of the government. He debated for commercial discrimination against Great Britain and for favorable trade with France and other nations. Madison was also instrumental in creating the executive and judicial departments, and in counseling President Washington on whom to consider for the posts.

Madison favored Alexander Hamilton as Secretary of the Treasury because of his business expertise. He also wanted Henry Knox to be the Secretary of War. He preferred that John Jay be the Chief Justice of the Supreme Court. And, he enticed Thomas Jefferson to come home from Paris, France to accept the post of Secretary of State. At President Washington's request, he also persuaded Edmund Randolph to accept the post of Attorney General.

Madison defended the authority of the President by pointing out that the chief executive had the right to terminate anyone from an executive office. Otherwise, he argued that the executive office would be encroached by the legislative department—instead of maintaining its executive independence. This presidential power, which was confirmed by the Senate, laid the cornerstone for what would become the most powerful executive office in the world.

Madison submitted a bill of rights to be added to the Constitution that would prohibit federal interference with personal liberties such as freedom of speech, trial by jury, and freedom of conscience. Out of hundreds proposed, Madison shortened it to a list of 145, and after summarizing these, submitted a list of 17 to the Congress. The House and Senate approved 12 of these for submittal to the states for ratification. Only 10 of these were approved by the states and these became the Bill of Rights.

Alexander Hamilton submitted a controversial plan for the federal government to assume all of the debts that had been incurred by the states during the Revolutionary War. To settle the issue, Madison proposed a compromise. Hamilton's proposal for the assumption of all debts by the government was agreed to by Jefferson in return for Hamilton's support in having the national capital be situated by the Potomac River.

In 1791, Madison wrote the State of the Union Address for President Washington. Madison also drafted the reply of the House to President Washington. Although Madison opposed the formation of a federal bank as proposed by Hamilton, the proposal was passed by the House. Madison was re-elected to the House in 1791. He published essays in the *National Gazette* on political economy in which he attacked the policies of Hamilton. He also urged President Washington to serve another term.

In 1793, when Thomas Jefferson resigned as Secretary of State, President Washington, offered the post to Madison, but he declined to serve. In January 1794, Madison introduced into the House 7 resolves on trade that were aimed against Great Britain—but was unsuccessful in getting these passed. In 1794, Madison was offered the post of envoy to France by President Washington, but he declined to serve. From 1796 to 1797, Madison participated in his last session in the House. He was unsuccessful in his effort to create a national university. He also consistently voted against defense appropriations and higher taxes,

Secretary of State

From 1797 to 1801, Madison was at his Montpelier mansion in Orange County, Virginia. In September 1794, Madison had married Dolley Payne Todd. Madison spent his time supervising the plantation that was worked by over 100 slaves. He stayed away from politics although he did participate with Thomas Jefferson in the drafting of the Virginia Resolutions in 1798—a response to the passing of the Alien and Sedition Acts during that year. Madison felt that these acts subverted the general principles of free government and the provisions of the Constitution, especially the First Amendment.

When Thomas Jefferson was elected as President in 1800, he chose Madison to be his Secretary of State. Because of ill health, Madison was not at Washington, D.C. until May 1801. In this position, Madison had many domestic duties including corresponding with governors, territorial officials, judges, marshals and attorneys. He also had to preserve public papers, print and distribute the laws, supervise the patent office, and keep track of the census. His foreign duties included corresponding with American ministers and with the many consuls around the world. He also had to deal with the foreign embassies in Washington, D.C., and with ordinary tasks such as issuing passports.

In 1801, Madison favored sending warships to the Mediterranean Sea to deal with the threat posed by Tripoli. In 1803, Madison supported the acquisition of Louisiana from France, and later helped plan the Lewis and Clark expedition. He also sought full possession of Florida from Spain. In 1805, Madison wrote *An Examination of the British Doctrine, Which Subjects to Capture a neutral Trade, Not Open in Time of Peace*, a pamphlet on international law, peace and free trade. In this tract he rejected the Rule of 1756, one established by the English Admiralty.

Election of 1808

In January 1808, Madison was chosen by a caucus to be the presidential candidate. In the December election of 1808, Madison won 122 Electoral votes and became President.

The First Term of James Madison

Events: 1809

<u>March 1809</u>

- In his Inaugural Address President Madison referred to the strained relationship between Great Britain and the United States, but he pledged to cultivate peace by observing justice and remaining neutral. However, he noted that because of belligerent powers—France and Great Britain—he was obligated to safeguard the nation against any threats. He also stressed that he would support the Constitution, foster a spirit of independence and protect all rights. He emphasized the need for an armed and trained militia as a bulwark to preserve the liberty of the republic. Finally, he appealed to the intelligence and virtue of his fellow citizens to aid him in caring for the national interests.
- President Madison's cabinet consisted as follows:
    - Secretary of State Robert Smith. In April 1811, President Madison fired his Secretary of State, Robert Smith. President Madison then appointed James Monroe as his new Secretary of State.
    - Secretary of the Treasury Albert Gallatin
    - Secretary of War William Eustis. In January 1813, President Madison appointed John Armstrong as Secretary of War to replace William Eustis.
    - Secretary of the Navy Paul Hamilton
    - Postmaster General Gideon Granger
    - Attorney General C. A. Rodney.

<u>April 1809</u>

- President Madison issued a proclamation that reinstituted trade between the United States and Great Britain.

<u>May 1809</u>

- President Madison addressed the Congress and expressed his wish to resume trading with Britain and France.

<u>June 1809</u>

- The House passed a bill to allocate $750,000 for defensive fortifications.
- The House presented a bill for action to secure an impartial jury in all civil and criminal cases maintained in the courts of the United States.

<u>August 1809</u>

- President Madison re-instated the Non-Intercourse Act against Great Britain and France.

- President Madison addressed the Congress to point out the belligerence of Great Britain. He also pointed out the belligerence of France in its trespassing of American commercial rights. He contrasted this situation with the existing amity with the Barbary powers.

Events: 1810

January 1810

- The House considered the American Navigation Bill, to prohibit the importation of British and French goods from neutral ports.
- The House authorized the President to employ armed vessels to protect commercial trade.
- The House authorized the President to detach troops to station them at the various frontier forts.
- A bill to engage a corps of volunteers, for a short period, in the service of the United States was considered by the Senate. This was the forerunner of the corps of volunteers that was popularized by President John Kennedy in the 1960s.

March 1810

- President Madison reported that 685,000 members of the militia existed in the states and territories.
- Chief Justice John Marshall of the Supreme Court handed down a decision in the case of *Fletcher v. Peck*. Marshall ruled in the claims arising from the Yazoo land fraud in Georgia that the original sale should be regarded as valid under the law of contracts. This became the first decision by the Supreme Court that nullified a state law on the basis of unconstitutionality. This ruling became the precedent for the right of the Supreme Court to declare acts of the states unconstitutional.
- Congress presented a provision to make by law the authorization of the President to cause the longitude of Washington, D. C. to be determined. The determination was to be made to the greatest degree of accuracy from the observatory located at Greenwich, England—and was to use the best available astronomical instruments in doing so.

April 1810

- The House passed a loan bill to cover the principal for the public debt.
- The House authorized the President to employ armed vessels to protect the commercial interests of the United States.

May 1810

- Congress ended the Non-intercourse Act, an action that removed all restrictions against trade with Britain and France. The new Macon Act authorized the President to re-instate non-intercourse against either nation in case the neutral commerce of the United States was violated by either of these powers.

July 1810

- President Madison attempted to deal with the problem of foreign occupation of West Florida by the Spanish. He asked Governor William Clairborne of the Orleans Territory whether the American settlers in West Florida should organize a convention to request a United States occupation.

September 1810

- American settlers in Spanish West Florida took possession of the western part in a rebellion against the Spanish rulers. The region between Baton Rouge and New Orleans was declared to be the Republic of West Florida. It then sought annexation by the United States. This was done in October 1810, when President Madison announced the annexation by the United States of the western portion of Spanish West Florida as part of the Territory of Orleans.

November 1810

- President Madison issued a proclamation opening up trade with France and halting it with Great Britain.

December 1810

- President Madison addressed the Congress and spoke about the commercial trade between the United States and Great Britain and France. He also talked about the problem with Spain concerning the Territory of West Florida. He addressed the uncertainties facing the United States, and thus he promoted the continuance of defensive arrangements, including naval expenditures.
- In the national census the population of the United States reached 7,240,000 inhabitants spread over 17 states.
- A committee was appointed to consider passing a law to prescribe the mode of taking evidence in cases of contested elections for members of the House of Representatives.
- The Committee of Commerce and Manufactures was instructed to inquire into the expediency of encouraging the culture of hemp by either protecting impost duties or by prohibiting the importation of that article into the United States.
- The House considered a bill from the Senate to make foreign gold coins be accepted as money and legal tender in the United States—but only for a period of 3 years.

- The Committee of Claims was authorized to inquire into the expediency of repealing or suspending the operation of several acts of limitation that barred the payment of claims against the United States held by valid certificates.

Events: 1811

January 1811

- A slave insurrection took place in Louisiana. More than 400 slaves revolted and marched on New Orleans where armed planters and soldiers killed 75 of them.
- Congress adopted a resolution that authorized the United States to extend its sovereignty over Spanish East Florida.
- The House considered an act to renew the incorporation of the Bank of the United States.
- A bill to conscript men aged 18 years and above for a limited term of service in the militia was defeated by the House.
- A bill to distribute arms to every citizen aged 18 and over was defeated by the House.

February 1811

- President Madison returned a bill incorporating the Protestant Episcopal Church in the town of Alexandria, Virginia back to the House. He did so because the bill exceeded the rightful authority to which the government was limited—and because it violated the First Amendment to the Constitution. The House reconsidered the bill, but this time it was soundly defeated.
- President Madison returned a bill that reserved a parcel of land of the United States for the use of a Baptist Church. He rejected it for the reason that it compromised a principle and precedent for appropriation of funds of the United States for the use and support of religious societies—an act contrary to the First Amendment to the Constitution.
- The House considered a revision of the patent laws that were considered inadequate to protect inventions.
- The Senate defeated the United States Bank charter renewal bill.

March 1811

- Congress voted to support the halting of trade with Great Britain.
- The Bank of the United States was dissolved.

May 1811

- The British frigate *Guerriere* seized the American brig *Spitfire* off the coast of New York, and impressed an American seaman. In retaliation, an American frigate, the *President*, disabled a British corvette, the *Little Belt*—an incident in which 9 British seamen were killed.

<u>November 1811</u>

- President Madison delivered a message to Congress in which he cited the trade grievances against Britain and France. He urged Congress to arm the United States to deal with the crisis. He also asked Congress to defray the expenses of government in light of decreasing revenues due to the effect of British actions on American shipping.
- The House urged an increase of 10,000 army personnel, 50,000 volunteers, the repairing of all American warships, and the arming of merchant ships.

<u>December 1811</u>

- Congress passed 6 resolves to accept war measures to resist the British actions.
- The House fixed the apportionment ratio for Representatives at 35,000 to 1.
- The Senate passed a bill that authorized the President to create companies of spies for the protection of the frontiers of the United States.

Events: 1812

<u>January 1812</u>

- Congress passed a bill that authorized the raising of an army of 25,000 men with a period of conscription of five years.
- The House defeated the bill for the expansion of the Navy. This action left the American Navy at a size of about one-sixth that of Great Britain's Navy.

<u>February 1812</u>

- Congress authorized President Madison to accept 50,000 militia from the states.
- The House recommended a list of war taxes on certain items to support military expenditures.

<u>March 1812</u>

- Congress authorized a bond for $11,000,000 to finance the military preparations that had been requested by President Madison.
- The House passed an embargo of 60 days to keep American ships beyond the reach of British warships.

<u>April 1812</u>

- Congress enacted into law an embargo for a period of 90 days.
- Congress empowered President Madison to call up 100,000 militia from the states for a period of service lasting 6 months.
- Louisiana became the 18th state in the Union.
- Vice President George Clinton died on April 20, 1812.

- President Madison returned a bill to the House concerning the absence or disability of judges in the United States district courts. He objected to the bill because it would have allowed Supreme Court judges to act as district court judges, and thus have the possibility of corroboration of judgments by the same person in those cases of appeal that might later reach the Supreme Court for a subsequent decision.

May 1812

- Congress incorporated the Republic of West Florida as part of the Mississippi Territory.

June 1812

- President Madison asked Congress for a declaration of war against Great Britain. The message addressed all of the British violations against American sovereignty and maritime grievances.
- British Minister Augustus Foster proposed a suspension of hostilities until a response was received from England to the American war declaration.
- Congress authorized $5,000,000 to finance the war.
- The House passed the declaration for war against Britain.
- The Senate passed the declaration for war against Britain. The Senate also authorized the President to invade Canada should it become necessary to do so.

July 1812

- Congress set increased tariffs on imports to help finance the war.

August 1812

- An emissary from the Governor General of Canada offered an armistice along the entire New York border, but it was rejected by the Madison administration. The British also rejected the peace proposals of American envoy Jonathan Russell.

September 1812

- The American government ignored the offer of armistice made by British Admiral Sir John Borlase Warren.
- President Madison issued a proclamation to the people of the United States asking them to unite in expelling the British invaders.

November 1812

- President Madison addressed the Congress with a message that focused on the war with Great Britain. In particular, he asked for forces to attack Canada and for protection of the frontier. He cited the recent American losses at Detroit, and the measures taken to create a superior naval force in the Great Lakes. He pointed out the American victories that had been achieved along the coast of the United States and on the Atlantic Ocean. To justify the declaration of war, he re-iterated the reasons for having taken such an action against Great Britain. Finally, he asked for an increase in the army, and for duties to support the war effort.

- The House passed a resolution to exempt soldiers from being arrested for debts that would therefore keep them out of service.

December 1812

- James Madison was reelected as President by an Electoral College vote of 128.

Events: 1813

January 1813

- The House considered a bill for raising an additional military force of 20,000 men for one year, thus adding to the 35,000 men that were already in the military.

February 1813

- Czar Alexander I of Russia offered to mediate the war between Great Britain and the United States—an offer that President Madison accepted.

March 1813

- President Madison took the oath of office from Chief Justice John Marshall.

The Second Term of James Madison

Events: 1813

March 1813

- In his Inaugural Address Madison addressed the war with Great Britain and pointed to the chief cause as being that of impressment of American sailors. He also mentioned the use of Indians by the British forces to inflict massacres, tortures, maiming and death on American settlers. He appealed to the patriotism, good sense and spirit of the citizens of the United States to share in the common burden, and to render the war short and victorious.
- President Madison had the following cabinet:
    - James Monroe as Secretary of State. In February 1814, President Madison appointed George W. Campbell as Secretary of State.
    - Albert Gallatin as Secretary of the Treasury. In December 1813, President Madison appointed George Campbell as Secretary of the Treasury. In September 1814, Secretary of the Treasury George Campbell resigned from office. In October 1814, President Madison appointed Alexander J. Dallas as his new Secretary of the Treasury. In October 1816, President Madison appointed William H. Crawford as Secretary of the Treasury.
    - John Armstrong as Secretary of War. In August 1814, President Madison asked for the resignation of John Armstrong as Secretary of War. President Madison then named James Monroe as acting Secretary of War.
    - William Jones as Secretary of the Navy. In December 1814, President Madison appointed Benjamin Crowninshield as the Secretary of the Navy.
    - Gideon Granger as Postmaster General. In December 1813, President Madison appointed Return Jonathan Meigs as Postmaster General.
    - William Pinkney as Attorney General. In December 1813, President Madison appointed Richard Rush as Attorney General.
    - President Madison sent peace commissioners in the mediation offered by Czar Alexander I.

May 1813

- The President addressed the Congress and spoke about the urgency of the war effort. He also told the Congress about the efforts of the Russian Czar to intercede in a peace negotiation with Great Britain. And, he appealed to the Congress for additional taxes to finance the war.

November 1813

- British Prime Minister Lord Castlereagh offered President Madison a negotiation for peace. President Madison accepted the offer and sent peace commissioners. The British, however, rejected the Czar's offer of mediation in the conflict.

- President Madison addressed the Congress in a State of the Union message. He cited the victories in the Great Lakes as proof of American naval superiority. At the end of the message he focused on the financial needs to keep the war effort going, and to keep the United States on course in its destiny to be a great, flourishing and powerful nation.

Events: 1814

January 1814

- Congress rejected Secretary of War Armstrong's call for conscription to enable President Madison to obtain 100,000 men. Instead the Congress enacted an enlistment bounty of 5 times the normal amount to entice men to join and fill the ranks of the army. It also authorized an army of almost 63,000 men.

March 1814

- President Madison recommended that the Congress repeal the Embargo and Non-Importation Acts.
- The House authorized a loan of $25,000,000.
- The House passed appropriations for the support of the United States Navy.
- The Senate debated the power of the President to make appointments for ambassadors to participate in the making of treaties. The issue was that these executive appointments had been made when the Senate was in recess.

April 1814

- Congress repealed the Embargo and Non-Importation Acts.

August 1814

- General William H. Winder attempted to defend the capital from the British attack by Admiral Sir George Cockburn and General Robert Ross. After an initial battle at Bladensburg, the American forces dispersed, and President Madison was forced to flee. Admiral Cockburn ordered his troops to torch the government buildings, including the White House and Capitol building.
- President Madison and his cabinet returned to Washington, D.C. Since the White House had been burned down, Madison used the Octagon House as his presidential mansion—a place where he lived until March 1817.

September 1814

- The Congress returned to Washington, D.C. and convened at the patent office building where it continued to meet until the end of 1815.

- President Madison addressed the Congress to inquire whether negotiations should be made with Great Britain to arrange for a return to peace, or if more effective provisions should be made instead to continue to prosecute the war. He cited the American victories, and he asked for more sums from taxes to meet the military expenses.

October 1814

- The British peace commissioners made demands for a negotiation in which the United States would give up Maine, remove all forts and warships from the Great Lakes area, give up fishing rights in the Newfoundland area, and create an Indian state that would act as a buffer between America and Canada. The American peace commissioners rejected this plan.
- Congress made a preliminary agreement to buy the library of Thomas Jefferson for use by the House and the Senate. The purchase, which cost $25,000, was made to replace the Congressional Library that had been destroyed by the British during the ransacking of the capital.

November 1814

- The cost to repair some of the damage to the public buildings that had been razed by the British forces was estimated by the House to be $1,215,000.

December 1814

- The House debated on the constitutionality of an apportionment of 80,000 men to be drafted from the various States and Territories.

Events: 1815

January 1815

- Congress passed a bill to create a Second National Bank, but President Madison vetoed the bill on Constitutional grounds.

February 1815

- President Madison declared the War of 1812 to be over with the ratification by the Senate and his signing of the Treaty of Ghent.
- The Senate failed to achieve a two-thirds vote to overturn President Madison's veto of the Second National Bank bill.

March 1815

- President Madison requested a standing army of 20,000 men.

- Congress passed legislation that authorized war against Algiers in retaliation for the plundering of American ships during the War of 1812. Congress also approved an act for the protection of the commerce of the United States against Algerian vessels.
- Congress authorized trade reciprocity with all nations.
- The Senate approved a standing army of 15,000.
- The House voted to set the number for a standing army to only 10,000.

May 1815

- Captain Stephen Decatur departed with a 10-ship fleet and headed towards the Mediterranean Sea to end the raids of the Barbary pirates on American ships.

June 1815

- Captain Stephen Decatur and his navy captured the Algerian frigate *Mashouda* and the Algerian brig *Estido*. After Captain Decatur threatened to bombard the city of Algiers, Algiers signed a treaty that ended hostilities against American shipping, agreed to free all American prisoners, and to end all demands for tribute payments from the American government.

December 1815

- President Madison addressed the Congress and requested a national public works program to build roads and canals. He also asked for improvements in the military forces, and for the establishment of a national university.
- President Madison announced a national debt of $120,000,000.

Events: 1816

January 1816

- The House introduced a bill for the creation of a Second Bank of the United States to be established in Philadelphia with branches in the various States.

March 1816

- In the case of *Martin v. Hunter's Lessee*, the Supreme Court ruled that it had the right to review state court decisions.

April 1816

- President Madison signed the bill passed by Congress for the creation of the Second National Bank of the United States.
- Congress passed the Tariff Act that set protective duties on imports ranging from 15 to 30 percent.

- A United States military expedition destroyed Fort Apalachicola in East Florida— a land held by the Spanish.

December 1816

- James Monroe was elected President with 183 Electoral votes.
- President Madison addressed the Congress and reported that the British were still denying entry to American ships in the West Indies. He asked Congress to retaliate against British trade. He cited that Spain had been warned against taking hostile action against American ships, and that Algiers would be dealt with force if he did not abide by the terms of the treaty that he had signed with the United States. He also asked for the establishment of a national university, for a reorganization of the militia, for a law against importation of slaves and for a modification of the Judiciary. Finally, he requested a decimal system of weights and measures, a liberalization of the criminal code, and the expediting of the discharge of the public debt that had already been substantially reduced.
- Indiana was admitted to the Union as the 19th state.
- The House proposed an alteration of the flag of the United States, given that four new states had been admitted to the Union without changing it[1].

Events: 1817

January 1817

- The Second Bank of the United States opened for business with a capitalization of $35,000,000.

February 1817

- Congress passed a bill that authorized public works projects, and set aside $1,500,000 for roads and canals.
- The House considered the American Society plan for colonizing free blacks and for abolishing the trafficking of slaves[2].

March 1817

- President Madison signed the Navigation Act that imposed the same restrictions on foreign ships as their home country imposed on American vessels.
- President Madison vetoed the public works bill that had been proposed by the House. The House attempted to override the veto, but could not get the necessary two-thirds approval, and so the bill was rejected.

Later Years

James Madison returned to his home at Montpelier, Virginia to become a planter. Despite his holdings, his debts mounted increasingly and he was forced to borrow to make ends meet. Madison saw the danger in the continuance of slavery, especially the incongruity and immorality in light of the principles of liberty and justice upon which the nation had been founded. Still, he failed in his attempt to free himself from the dependency on slave labor, as well as in his efforts to secure a law for gradual abolition in Virginia.

He did foresee the unalterable prejudices that would exist if blacks were to be incorporated into the white population, especially for meaningful freedom and equality. Thus, he argued for a relocation of blacks in either the American West—or in thinly settled parts of West Africa—in order to maintain a division of separate societies that would allow blacks both freedom and opportunity, as well as a safe haven from the inherent superiority prejudices of the white society. To this end, he joined with others in founding the American Colonization Society—an organization dedicated to freeing the slaves and to transporting them to the west coast of Africa[3].

In 1816, Madison was appointed as a trustes of the University of Virginia. In 1829, Madison was elected as a delegate to participate in the drafting of a new state constitution for Virginia. His main contribution was to extend the vote to all householders and heads of families who paid taxes.

In 1829, Madison calculated a future for America in 1929 that would be comprised of 192,000,000 people. His vision included a prophetic situation of teeming cities filled with day laborers, and a countryside of very few farmers.

Madison was in poor health and suffered from rheumatism. From 1835 to 1836, he was afflicted with fever and fatigue. On June 28, 1836, James Madison died at Montpelier, Virginia at the age of 85.

Legacy

During Madison's first term, guiding the War of 1812 was his most important mission as President. In spite of opposition to the war, he was re-elected and Madison was able to emerge with a newfound popularity after the Treaty of Ghent and General Andrew Jackson's victory at New Orleans. During his second term, he was successful in the creation of the Second Bank of the United States. This financial institution proved to be of great value, especially in helping the nation survive the Panic of 1819. Madison also promoted a moderate tariff to protect the infant industries in America from foreign competition. He never wavered from his stance of the complete separation of church and state, he championed cooperative power to bring about social justice, and he adhered to liberty as the only way to open up the opportunities and potential of humanity to everyone.

Endnotes

1   The current flag had 15 stripes and 15 stars and did not show that there were 19 states in the United States. Since it was determined that it was inexpedient to change the number of stripes due to size considerations, the House committee suggested that to prevent future extensive alterations that only a star be added for each additional state that was brought into the Union. It also recommended a change to revert to the original thirteen stripes as a symbol of the beginning of independence in the United States.

2   It was considered inexpedient and very difficult to place the free blacks in Sierra Leone—a country in Africa that was being used by Great Britain to relocate the slaves from America that it had captured during the Revolutionary War. An alternative to the proposal to relocate freed slaves in Sierra Leone was to create a separate colony on the west coast of Africa under the auspices of the United States.

3   The American Society was responsible for founding Liberia in 1822, as a nation for freed American slaves in the west coast of Africa, with its capital being named Monrovia by the society in honor of James Monroe. The country of Liberia is situated next to Sierra Leone, a nation that became settled by Great Britain with former slaves from America.

James Monroe

The Fifth President Under the Constitution

Early Years

James Monroe was born in Westmoreland County, Virginia on April 28, 1758. His father was Spence Monroe, and his mother was Elizabeth Jones. His education began when he enrolled at Campbelltown Academy in 1769 where he studied Latin and mathematics. In 1774, his father died, and Monroe left the Academy to enroll at William and Mary College. As the Revolutionary conflict widened, Monroe joined a group of 24 men in a raid on the British Governor's palace where they captured muskets and swords for the Williamsburg militia.

Military Service

In 1776, Monroe left William and Mary College and enlisted as a cadet in the Third Virginia Infantry. He became a lieutenant, and in 1777, his regiment joined General George Washington's Army on Long Island. He was with an advance detachment of 50 men when General Washington conducted the attack on the Hessian Army at Trenton, New Jersey by crossing the Delaware River in 1777. Monroe was seriously wounded in the shoulder in a charge against Hessian soldiers who were trying to mount two cannons to use against the approaching American forces. An artery that had been severed by a bullet was plugged by a doctor, thus preventing Monroe from bleeding to death.

Monroe was promoted to the rank of Captain. He accepted the post of aide-de-camp with the rank of Major under General William Alexander. He was also with General George Washington at Valley Forge during the terrible winter between 1778 and 1779. He participated at the Battles of Brandywine and Monmouth—in the latter playing an important part as head of a scouting party. However, this was his last engagement in military service during the Revolutionary War except for a brief period in 1780 when he acted as a military agent for Governor Thomas Jefferson of Virginia to establish a system of expresses to transmit messages.

Second Continental Congress: 1783-1786

In 1780, Monroe re-entered William and Mary College where he studied law. In 1782, he was elected as a delegate to the Virginia House of Delegates. He then served on the Governor's Council, and seized the opportunity to make extensive investments of 100,000 acres in western lands.

In 1783, Monroe was selected to attend the Second Continental Congress as a delegate. He attended the Second Continental Congress and in 1784, he was on a committee that was appointed to revise the system of the War Office. He was also on a committee that created the instructions for the American Minister to Spain to represent the claims of the

United States according to the Treaty of Paris that had been signed with Great Britain. He supported Thomas Jefferson's Land Ordinance of 1784.

In 1785, he dealt with many of the petitions from inhabitants of Canada who had become refugees as a result of having supported the United States during the Revolutionary War. He was a member of the Grand Committee in which he participated in the propositions regarding the coinage of gold, silver and copper, and on the matter of the national debt. He favored permitting Congress to regulate commerce, with the imposts being both collected and spent by the states. And, he was on a committee that recommended a resolution to disqualify members of Congress from being appointed to any office or trust under the United States.

In 1786, Monroe participated on numerous committees concerned with revenue generation. He was on a committee tasked with advising the United States Department of Foreign Affairs in the negotiations and measures to be taken with the Barbary powers. Monroe also formulated the Land Ordinance of 1787.

State Legislator

In February 1786, Monroe married Elizabeth Kortright. He opened a law office in Fredericksburg, Virginia, but financial difficulties plagued him, and he was forced to sell several slaves to avoid being forced into bankruptcy. In 1786, he lost the election for the House of Delegates, but in 1787, he won the election to be a member of the House. Although he was chosen to attend the Annapolis Convention of 1786, Monroe was passed over when the selections were made to attend the Constitutional Convention in Philadelphia in 1787. In 1787, he promoted the resolutions that called for the repeal of all laws that were impeding the collection of British debts.

In 1788, Monroe participated as a delegate in the state ratification convention of the United States Constitution. Monroe did approve of the structure of the proposed government, especially the effective compromise between local and national governments. He was also against the makeup of the Senate because of its principle of state equality, and he deemed it unwise for the Senate to share in executive powers. He was against the granting of the power to levy direct taxes. He recommended that the federal government be given direct control over the militia. To maintain a strong leadership, Monroe favored the veto power of the executive, and the strict limitation on Congress for treaty-making power. He wanted the consent of two-thirds of the Senate for any commercial treaty, and the consent of three-fourths of both houses for any treaty yielding territory or navigational rights.

Monroe approved of Amendments as a way of strengthening the Constitution, and protested the omission of a Bill of Rights. His most important objection was to the Electoral College. He thought that this system would make the President subservient to state interests, and that it opened the door to manipulation and bribery by those seeking to control the government. Thus, he preferred that the people directly elect the President of the United States. When the vote for ratification took place, Monroe voted against the Constitution.

United States Senator

In 1789, Monroe ran for a seat in Congress, but lost. In 1790, Monroe ran for the Senate and won the election. During the first session of the Senate, Monroe was a member of nearly all of the important committees. Monroe voted against the incorporation of The Bank of the United States in 1791. Monroe also opposed the Washington administration in its plans to enlarge the Army for the protection of the West.

Minister to France

President Washington appointed Monroe in 1794 as Minister to France. Monroe sailed for France aboard the *Cincinnatus*, and arrived at La Havre, France in July 1794. Guided by his desire to command French esteem and to secure their cooperation, he pursued a course that was at odds with what the State Department wanted. He raised the question of indemnities from the embargo placed on American ships, presented a demand by American merchants, and raised the issue of why France was not adhering to the principles of the Treaty of 1788. Monroe was reprimanded for his actions, and was eventually recalled in 1796. Monroe stayed behind and did not depart from France until 1797, arriving in Philadelphia aboard the *Amity* in June 1797.

Governor of Virginia

Monroe returned to his law practice in Virginia while he decided what to do next. In 1799, he was elected as governor. As Governor he pleaded for the establishment of a state-supported educational system. He also wanted a well-trained militia to provide for the national defense. Although Monroe shared a conviction that slavery was evil, he did not favor abolition and thought that the institution of slavery had to be maintained until another solution could be found.

The legislature authorized the Governor to investigate the possibility of buying territory in the West to which dangerous persons could be shipped to. When Monroe asked Thomas Jefferson for advice, Jefferson offered to investigate the possibility of a refuge for slaves somewhere in Africa. He suggested Sierra Leone, a colony that had been founded by the British as a refuge for slaves who had been captured and removed from America. However, the English did not agree to this proposal, and subsequently all slaves who were convicted of crimes were instead kept in prison.

Envoy to France

At the end of his third term as Governor in 1802, Monroe decided to practice law in Richmond, Virginia. He declined a nomination to the state chancery court, and he declined to accept a position as United States Senator. In 1803, Monroe was chosen by President Thomas Jefferson as an Envoy Extraordinary to France in the effort to purchase

New Orleans from the French. After receiving instructions to purchase New Orleans and Florida for the sum of $2,000,000, Monroe departed for France aboard the *Richmond*, reaching the port of Le Havre in April 1803, from where he traveled to Paris, France.

By this time Robert Livingston, the other minister to France, had already reached an implied agreement with the French by which all of Louisiana was to be purchased by the United States. Thus, Monroe found his welcome by Livingston less than enthusiastic. In fact, Livingston did not inform Monroe of this event until he realized that they both must act before Napoleon changed his mind about selling the entire territory. Finally, an agreement was reached in April 1803 in which the United States agreed to pay $15,000,000 for the land and the liquidation of claims against France. However, there was only a verbal assurance that France would support the United States in its negotiations with Spain over Florida—a territory that was assumed to be included in the Louisiana Purchase.

Minister to England

Monroe remained in France until July 1803, and then departed for England to take up his post as Minister. Later that year he traveled to Paris, France to discuss with the French the commitment that he had verbally made concerning the territory of Florida. However, the French now endorsed the Spanish claim that West Florida had never been part of the Louisiana Territory. In 1804, Monroe traveled to Madrid, Spain to engage in specific discussions over the contested territory of West Florida. But, President Jefferson was not inclined to pursue the matter since he did not consider Florida to be of vital interest to the United States.

Monroe visited Madrid, Spain once again in 1805 for further talks about West Florida. He met with the Prime Minister who stated that the American claims were unreasonable. The Spanish protracted the negotiations and refused to relinquish anything—to the point that it caused the termination of the negotiations. Monroe then returned to London, England in July 1805. A treaty that Monroe worked out with England was rejected by President Jefferson because it lacked a ban on impressment. Subsequently, Monroe set sail to America in November 1807.

Governor of Virginia

Monroe arrived at Norfolk, Virginia in December 1807, where he was encouraged to run for the presidential nomination. However, he was defeated in the preliminary election of Virginia. In 1810, he was elected to the Virginia Legislature. He then ran for the governorship of Virginia and won. However, Monroe served as Governor of Virginia for only 3 months until March 1811. He was then offered the position of Secretary of State by President Madison, which he accepted.

Secretary of State

As Secretary of State, Monroe became involved with preparations for war against England. He worked closely with the Committee of Foreign Affairs in the House. Monroe proposed the enactment of a 60-day embargo against British goods, which President Madison then requested from Congress. To get the required Congressional approval for war, a manifesto was drafted by Monroe for a war declaration. The House approved of the declaration of war against England. The Senate debated the same declaration and it too voted for war.

Acting Secretary of War

In December 1812, Monroe was appointed as the acting Secretary of War. Monroe called for an expansion of the army by 50,000 volunteers plus 20,000 additional regulars. In 1813, Monroe submitted a report to Congress that advocated the occupation of all Florida as a war measure, but the Congress declined to approve this action. Consequently, American troops were withdrawn from Spanish territory in May 1813.

Monroe stepped aside in February 1813, to allow John Armstrong to be appointed as the new Secretary of War. Monroe was then considered for an appointment into the army as a Brigadier General, but he refused. When a 3-man peace delegation to England was created by President Madison in April 1813, it was Monroe who devised the instructions for the 3 envoys.

Monroe wanted a communication system based on a chain of expresses to be set up along the Chesapeake Bay to provide intelligence on enemy army movements. Secretary of War John Armstrong refused to admit the possibility of the capital being attacked and thus did not act on this measure. Monroe kept insisting, and finally President Madison established a new military district that included the Potomac River and Chesapeake Bay.

Still, President Madison did not feel the urgency that Monroe had about the possibility of invasion of the capital city. Consequently, the British marched towards Washington. D.C. Secretary of War Armstrong failed to act as British forces marched to Blandensburg. An American force of over 7,000 men was driven back by a British force that numbered only 4,000 men—without any artillery or cavalry. Then, the British ransacked the city of Washington, D.C., burning the President's House and many of the government office buildings. President Madison asked Monroe to assume command of the defenses of the city of Washington, D.C. Monroe became Secretary of War again when President Madison entered his named to the Senate, which confirmed Monroe as the Secretary of War.

Monroe directed his focus toward the preparation of the defense of Baltimore where the British headed next. He raised troops, summoned the militia, assembled supplies and set up an intelligence system. He placed General Samuel Smith in charge of the defense of Baltimore—a task that he was able to perform by defeating the British at Fort McHenry in September 1814. In September 1814, Monroe sent a letter to General Andrew Jackson to warn him of the British threat at New Orleans. In October 1814, Monroe requested the creation of a conscript army of 100,000 men. Monroe also borrowed over $5,000,000 from various banks and municipal corporations.

In February 1815, Monroe drafted a report that was submitted to the for a peacetime military establishment. Monroe's recommendation was for a standing army of 20,000 men to be maintained on a permanent basis, and an additional force of 35,000 regulars to guard the borders at Canada and Florida. Monroe served as Secretary of War until March 1815.

Return to the State Department

Monroe returned to his duties as Secretary of State in March 1815. He instructed the peace commissioners who were dealing with Algeria to obtain the complete security for American ships without the payment of any tribute. In the military expedition headed by Commodore Stephen Decatur, a secured treaty was obtained that was in full accordance with Monroe's edicts. In July 1816, Monroe began talks with the British to demilitarize the Great Lakes area. The culmination of these talks was the Rush-Bagot Treaty of 1817.

Election as President

Monroe became a contender for the Presidency in 1816. Monroe won the Congressional caucus nomination, and won the Presidential election of 1816 with 183 Electoral College votes. On March 4, 1817, President James Monroe took the oath of office from Chief Justice John Marshall.

The First Term of James Monroe

Events: 1817

March 1817

- In his Inauguration Address, President Monroe expressed his support for a standing Army to protect American citizens, and an adequate Navy to protect the country's maritime interests. He suggested the creation of coastal fortifications. He also stressed the need to maintain a strong central government, to protect American industry and to formulate a program to encourage industry, trade and commerce. President Monroe addressed the improvement of the roads and canals in order to adequately connect the various parts of the country. However, most of his message was concerned with the happy condition of the United States that currently existed—although the War of 1812 had resulted in a debt of $120,000,000. He ended his message with a stated intention to promote peace abroad and at home.
- President Monroe's cabinet consisted as follows:
    - John Quincy Adams as Secretary of State
    - William H. Crawford as Secretary of the Treasury
    - Isaac Shelby as Secretary of War. In 1817, John C. Calhoun accepted the post.
    - Benjamin W. Crowninshield as Secretary of the Navy. When he resigned, President Monroe appointed Smith Thompson to replace him.
    - R. J. Meigs as Postmaster General
    - Richard Rush as Attorney General—who was later replaced by William Wirt.

April 1817

- The Rush-Bagot Agreement was signed by the United States and the British. The agreement prevented a naval armaments race between the two countries by limiting the number of naval vessels on the Great Lakes.

December 1817

- Mississippi entered the Union as the 20th state.
- President Monroe addressed Congress in his State of the Union speech. He cited the reduction of naval forces on the Great Lakes in a mutual agreement with Great Britain. He mentioned that the trade agreements made with Great Britain were still unresolved, and that the negotiations with Spain over the disputed lands in Florida were currently suspended. Monroe asked for the repeal of internal taxes as he thought that taxes on imports and the sale of public lands would generate enough revenue to meet the needs of the government. Finally, President Monroe expressed the need to institute a public works program.

- President Monroe ordered General Edmund Gaines to start operations against the Seminole Indians in Florida with full authority to pursue them into Spanish territory—although he was not to attack them if they took refuge in a Spanish post. Since General Gaines was not available, the command of the United States expeditionary forces was instead given to General Andrew Jackson.

Events: 1818

January 1818

- General Andrew Jackson communicated to President Monroe that he could capture Spanish Florida for the United States within 60 days. President Monroe gave a tacit approval to General Jackson, who thus began a 60-day military campaign.
- A proposal to increase the compensation to members of Congress to $1,500 per year was defeated in the House.
- A bill was passed by the House to increase the rate of pay for each member to $8 for each day spent in session, and mileage of $8 per trip to and from a session from their home state.

February 1818

- An expatriation bill was considered by the House to deprive a citizen of the United States of his right to that citizenship. The condition for expatriation was to be based on a person relinquishing their status as a citizen and departing out of the United States. However, the bill was rejected.

March 1818

- Congress passed the first Pension Act to provide lifetime pensions for veterans of the Revolutionary War.
- The House agreed to the proposal for the expatriation of an American citizen.
- The House voted that Congress had the right to appropriate money for the construction of roads, canals and other watercourses.

April 1818

- Congress passed a resolution that limited the number of stripes on the American flag to the original 13. It also ordered that a new star be added to the flag for each new state that was admitted to the Union.
- The House considered a proposal from the Society of Friends for the African colonization of freed slaves from the United States. In a resolution that was passed, the President of the United States was requested to ascertain whether a suitable territory could be procured on the west coast of Africa for such colonization.

May 1818

- General Andrew Jackson seized St. Marks and Pensacola, Florida and forced the Spanish Governor and his soldiers to depart for Havana, Cuba.
- President Monroe agreed to keep American forces in Florida until Spain provided adequate garrisons. They also agreed to instruct American Ministers to declare that the United States would regard with hostility any interference in Latin America—a precursor event before the Monroe Doctrine was declared in 1823.

October 1818

- The American Ministers signed the Convention of 1818 agreement with England. This pact clarified the settlement that was reached by the Treaty of Ghent in 1814, including fixing the border between Canada and the United States at the 49th parallel in the Oregon region.

November 1818

- Secretary of State John Quincy Adams informed Spain that General Jackson's expedition into Florida had been an act of self-defense because of the Indian attacks. Adams also informed Spain that it should cede this area to the United States if it was incapable of controlling it.
- President Monroe addressed the Congress and stated his wish for continued relations with Great Britain. He also stated his concerns with Spain in regard to the situation in Florida. And, he briefly touched on the current economic state of affairs in the United States. His suggestion for financial affairs was the repeal of all internal taxes that had been levied during the War of 1812.

December 1818

- Illinois was admitted as the 21st state into the Union.

Events: 1819

January 1819

- A financial panic occurred as a result of curtailment of credit, and because of a Congressional order mandating payments to be done with hard currency only. The panic caused the collapse of state banks, and led to the foreclosure of large tracts of real estate. The depression was compounded by overexpansion of credit, the collapse of the export market, low-priced imports from Europe, widespread unemployment and unsound banking policies that created financial instability.

February 1819

- The Adams-Onis Treaty with Spain was signed and ratified by the Senate. By the terms of the treaty Spain ceded East Florida to the United States, and renounced claims to West Florida, which was already annexed by the United States. In return, the United States renounced its claims to Texas.
- Supreme Court Chief Justice John Marshall ruled in the case of *Trustees of Dartmouth College v. Woodward* that a private charter is a contract and cannot be broken or revised by a state.
- The Supreme Court ruled in the case of *Sturges v. Crowninshield* that a state bankruptcy law that was passed after the sealing of a contract violated the contract clause of the United States Constitution.

March 1819

- Chief Justice John Marshall of the Supreme Court ruled in the case of *McCulloch v. Maryland* that a state may not tax an agency of the United States, including the federal bank. The court also upheld the right of Congress to create the Bank of the United States under the implied powers clause of the Constitution.
- Congress passed an immigration law that mandated lists of passengers that were to be provided by captains on each voyage.

December 1819

- Alabama entered the Union as the 22nd state.
- President Monroe addressed the Congress in which he spoke about the merits of the treaty with Spain. He also addressed the differences between Great Britain and the United States with respect to the interpretation of the Treaty of Ghent that had been agreed to in 1815. Finally, he talked about providing encouragement and protection to domestic manufacturers by a higher protective tariff.

Events: 1820

March 1820

- Maine was admitted as the 23rd state into the Union.

April 1820

- Congress passed the Public Land Act that reduced the minimum price to $1.25 per acre and the minimum size of purchase of western lands to 80 acres.
- The House submitted a manufacturing and protective tariff bill, but iy was defeated in the Senate.

May 1820

- Congress passed the Tenure of Office Act that limited the length of specified political appointments to a term of 4 years. The act was geared towards federal officials whose duties involved financial responsibilities.

<u>November 1820</u>

- President Monroe addressed the Congress and cautioned that the nation should remain vigilant, especially against foreign wars from Europe that might threaten the state of peace in America. He mentioned the negotiations and relations with Spain, France, Britain, and the Barbary Coast Powers, especially with regard to the treaties and policies that had been formulated by the United States with each of these nations. With regard to the national debt, President Monroe stated that it had been reduced by nearly $68,000,000 from its original amount of almost $159,000,000.

<u>December 1820</u>

- The fourth census showed the population of the United States to be 9,600,000 people.
- President Monroe was reelected by receiving 231 Electoral votes.

Events: 1821

<u>January 1821</u>

- The Senate considered the expediency of settlements along the Columbia River by the Pacific Ocean.

<u>February 1821</u>

- The Senate considered a resolution as to which officer would act as President and Vice President in case of vacancies in both offices.

<u>March 1821</u>

- The Supreme Court in the case of *Cohens v. Virginia* reaffirmed the previous ruling in 1816 in the case of *Martin v. Hunter's Lessee* that it had the authority to review decisions of the state courts.
- Congress passed the Relief Act that permitted price adjustments for western land purchases that were unpaid for.
- President Monroe took the oath of office from Chief Justice John Marshall.

The Second Term of James Monroe

Events: 1821

<u>March 1821</u>

- In his Inaugural Address President Monroe spoke about the successful end to the War of 1812. He also referred to a reduced peacetime army and navy that would still be large enough to defend the coasts and lands of the United States. With regard to the emerging nations in South America, and their break away from European colonization through revolutions, President Monroe recommended a policy of neutrality. However, he also noted that the United States would always have the power to take other measures—especially if events affected its national interests. Still, he mentioned the acquisition of Florida as an unfortunate set of occurrences that resulted from what he regarded as piratical activities by participants from the United States. But, he acknowledged the events that transpired and the subsequent treaty with Spain had prevented worse consequences from happening. President Monroe cited the agreements with Great Britain, which fixed the northwest boundary between the United States and British North America. And, he stated the success of holding the Barbary Powers in check through the use of a strong naval force. President Monroe addressed the financial situation of the United States by pointing out that nearly $67,000,000 of the public debt had been paid. He also justified the action of floating loans as a means of obtaining revenue rather than resorting to more internal taxation. But, he noted that in times of great emergencies it might be necessary to impose internal taxes as a means of augmenting revenue. In terms of foreign policy, President Monroe stated his conviction to have a strong peacetime preparedness— something that he felt was essential for the nation's safety. He also proclaimed the strength of the United States, and its newfound position as a great power in the world. In support of this view he stated that the United States had complete sovereignty over a very large tract of territory from which new states were being added to the Union. And, he emphasized this view by noting that the population of the country had extended in all directions, something that represented a force of powerful dimensions and faculties—without necessarily having to invoke the capacity of oppressing other peoples.
- President Monroe retained his entire cabinet from his previous administration, which was as follows:
    - John Quincy Adams as Secretary of State
    - William H. Crawford as Secretary of the Treasury
    - John C. Calhoun as Secretary of War
    - Smith Thompson as Secretary of the Navy
    - R. J. Meigs as Postmaster General
    - William Wirt as Attorney General.

- President Monroe appointed General Andrew Jackson to be the first Governor of Florida.

- Missouri was admitted into the Union as the 24th state.

- President Monroe addressed the Congress and spoke about reciprocal trade agreements between the United States and European countries, and the status of favored nation concessions. He talked about the current financial condition of the country in light of the recent economic depression that had occurred. Finally, he emphasized the need to maintain a naval force in the Pacific Ocean to protect the commercial interests of the United States.

Events: 1822

- The House approved an apportionment bill to raise the existing limit of 35,000 inhabitants per Representative, but could not agree on the specific number.
- The House proposed a plan for the reorganization of the Army.

- The House agreed to a reapportionment of Representatives to be done according to the results of the 1820 census of the United States.

- In a precursor declaration to the Monroe Doctrine, President Monroe sent a special message to the Congress that proposed recognition by the United States for 5 new Latin American Republics who had recently achieved independence:
  - Colombia
  - Peru
  - Argentina
  - Mexico
  - Chile.

- The House approved a bill from the Senate providing for a government for Florida.
- The House agreed on resolutions to support South American governments in their quest for freedom from the European interests.

- The Senate considered a bill to establish a government for the Territory of Florida, but voted against annexation.
- The Senate rejected a resolution to limit the number of Representatives in the House to a total of 200 members.

April 1822

- Congress passed the Cumberland Road Tolls Bill that instituted a system of tolls for the repair of the Cumberland Road.
- The House defeated a revised compensation bill for its members, those of the Senate, and the executive staff.
- The House passed a bill to support the upkeep of the Cumberland Road. It included a provision that authorized the President to collect a toll on a section of that road if a particular state in which that section was located failed to maintain it and perform repairs on it.

May 1822

- President Monroe vetoed the Cumberland Road Tolls bill on the grounds that the government lacked jurisdiction over public improvements.

July 1822

- President Monroe sent a diplomatic note to the Russian Czar protesting the Russian claim to the Pacific Northwest. The note threatened the possibility of war if Russia attempted to assume physical control of that region. Secretary of State John Quincy Adams reasserted this position by informing the Russian Minister to the United States that the American continents were no longer open to any European colonial establishments.

October 1822

- The Erie Canal that linked Rochester and Albany, New York was opened.

December 1822

- President Monroe addressed the Congress in a message that urged the removal of duties and restrictions on both British and French ships. Monroe affirmed the ceding of Florida by Spain to the United States in accordance with the treaty with Spain. In domestic affairs, he advocated the passage of an Amendment that would legally allow the government to pursue the construction of roads, canals and other public works. In foreign affairs, he vowed to pursue the cause of liberty and humanity.

- The House requested that the President inform it of any hostile action or expedition against Puerto Rico which may have been planned in the United States.
- The House also agreed to consider a bill to authorize the occupation of the mouth of the Columbia River.
- The House considered the fortification of Key West in Florida as a protection against the Spanish who were in Havana, Cuba.

Events: 1823

January 1823

- The House defeated the bill to authorize the occupation of the mouth of the Columbia River.
- The motion to pursue an expedition of the Artic and Antarctic regions of the earth was defeated by the House.

February 1823

- The Supreme Court ruled in the case of *Green v. Biddle* that a contract between two states is just as valid as a contract between two private parties.
- The House passed a bill making the gold coins of Great Britain, France, Portugal and Spain receivable as payments for land transactions.

July 1823

- The *Beagle* under the command of Commodore Porter's piracy suppression squadron in the West Indies, in company with the *Greyhound* landed a party at Cape Cruz, Cuba and broke up the headquarters of a pirate band.

September 1823

- The Champlain Canal that linked the Hudson River in New York with Lake Champlain was opened.

December 1823

- President Monroe addressed the Congress with a message concerned with the security of Americans and the relations with foreign powers. He noted the disagreements between Great Britain and the United States over the boundaries of territories that were claimed by both. He cited a projected surplus in the Treasury of almost $9,000,000 by the end of 1824. President Monroe also mentioned the need to increase the tariff to protect American industry, and the turning over of the Cumberland Road to the states so that tolls could be collected for its maintenance. President Monroe announced the principles that would become known as the Monroe Doctrine. The message proclaimed to the entire world that the American continents were free and independent, and that they were not to be considered as subjects for future colonization by any European powers. Thus, any European intervention in the Western Hemisphere would be viewed as a manifestation of an unfriendly disposition toward the United States.

- The Senate produced a count and amount of Revolutionary War pensions as reported by the states. The account showed that 14,000 pensioners had received a combined amount of $1,334,000.

Events: 1824

<u>January 1824</u>

- The House passed a resolution that determined the maximum award in damages for costs involving patent cases in which the plaintiff lost. The bill provided for double damages in terms of costs incurred by the defendant.

<u>March 1824</u>

- The Supreme Court ruled in the case of *Gibbons v. Ogden* that a monopoly granted by the New York Legislature for steamboat navigation was unconstitutional because only the Federal Government has jurisdiction over interstate commerce.
- The Supreme Court ruled in the case of *Osborn v. Bank of the United States* that a state couldn't tax a federal corporation.

<u>April 1824</u>

- The United States and Russia signed a treaty that placed the limit of Russia's claim in the Pacific Northwest to the parallel line defined by 54^0 40' as well as removing the ban on all commercial shipping of other nations in its territorial waters.

<u>May 1824</u>

- Congress adopted a Tariff Act, which imposed severe duties on imports.

<u>June 1824</u>

- The Supreme Court ruled in the case of *Bank of the United States v. Planter's Bank of Georgia* that a state that becomes a party to any banking or business venture is subject to liability for a legal suit as part of that commercial venture.

<u>November 1824</u>

- Commodore David Porter led 200 sailors from the ship *Beagle* in an attack on the Puerto Rican town of Fajardo in pursuit of a pirate band. This invasion of Spanish sovereignty resulted in the recall and court-martial of Commodore Porter.

<u>December 1824</u>

- President Monroe addressed the Congress in a message that forecast a deficit if imports continued to decline. But, he endorsed the increase in the tariff that had been passed by Congress because it afforded protection to the American manufacturers.
- In the presidential election of 1824, no candidate received a majority, thus throwing the election into the House again for resolution.

Events: 1825

<u>February 1825</u>

- The House resolved the presidential election by choosing John Quincy Adams as President.

<u>March 1825</u>

- John Adams was given the otah of office of the Presidency by Chief Justice John Marshall.

Later Years

James Monroe moved back to his home in Virginia where he enjoyed outdoor pursuits such as horseback riding. He worked to increase the return from his plantings of grains such as wheat and rye on his estate. He resisted any further involvement in political activities, and he turned down President Adam's offer to go on a mission to the Panama Congress in 1826. He also declined to accept a nomination for Vice President on the Adams ticket of 1828.

Monroe pursued claims that he had made against the government for reimbursement for past services related to his transactions over the past 30 years. His initial claim was equal to $53,000, but eventually he was paid $30,000 by the Congress in February 1831. He still owed the Bank of the United States $25,000, which was part of a total debt of $75,000 on his 3,500-acre estate at Albemarle. He eventually turned over 2,800 acres to the Bank of the United States to discharge the debt of $25,000.

Monroe spent much of his leisure in his library, which contained approximately 3,000 volumes. Monroe also began work on an autobiography. Monroe's last public service was as a member of the Virginia constitutional convention in 1829. He fought for enlarging the suffrage, and insisted only on a minimal land ownership requirement for the privilege of voting. In September 1830, his wife Elizabeth died. Since old age infirmities had finally overcome him, Monroe moved to New York in 1830. James Monroe died on July 4, 1831, in New York City.

Legacy

Monroe spent his entire lifetime in a dedicated effort of strengthening the United States. His contributions began during the Revolutionary War, then continued at the Confederation Congress, and finally ended at the federal level as a Cabinet member and then President. In foreign affairs, Monroe got an agreement from Spain to cede Florida, an agreement from the British to define the Northwest boundary, and an agreement from Russia to define the Pacific Coast boundary. In domestic affairs, Monroe had to deal with the Panic of 1819, the first depression that occurred in the United States, and with the issue of slavery that resulted in the Missouri Compromise of 1820. Monroe also made many improvements in the construction of roads and canals as well as lighthouses. 5 new states were admitted to the Union during his Presidency: Alabama, Illinois, Maine, Mississippi and Missouri. Monroe is remembered for his Monroe Doctrine declaration in 1823, which warned the European powers against intervention in the Western Hemisphere.

John Quincy Adams

The Sixth President Under the Constitution

Early Years

John Quincy Adams was born at Braintree, Massachusetts on July 11, 1767. His father was John Adams, the second Constitutional President of the United States. His mother was Abigail Smith. He received his education by instruction from his father and mother. In 1778, he accompanied his father on the frigate *Boston* for diplomatic missions to Europe. When they arrived at Bordeaux, France, they then journeyed to Paris, France. Adams was placed in a private boarding school, and there he studied French. He also studied Latin, fencing, dancing, drawing and music.

When his father was recalled by the Continental Congress, they both sailed back to America on the French frigate, *La Sensible*, in 1779. After arriving at Braintree, Massachusetts, his father was again chosen to go to Paris, France to seek a treaty of peace and commerce with Great Britain. They set sail once more on the *Sensible*, and arrived in El Ferrol, Spain in December 1779. Traveling by land, they arrived in Paris, France in February 1780. John entered a pension academy where he studied Greek, Latin, geography, mathematics, drawing and writing.

When his father moved to Holland to persuade the Dutch government to recognize the American independence, Adams enrolled in the Latin school in Amsterdam, Holland in September 1780. In January 1781, Adams was accepted as a student at the University of Leyden in Amsterdam, Holland where he studied medicine, chemistry, philosophy, Greek and Latin. In July 1781, Adams left the university to accompany Francis Dana who had been appointed to conduct diplomatic negotiations with Russia at St. Petersburg. He was selected for the position of secretary and interpreter of French, which was the official language of the Russian Court. Traveling through Berlin, Germany, they arrived in St. Petersburg in August 1781. Adams kept his academic studies by searching through bookstores for volumes that interested him, and he refined his mastery of the French language while also studying German.

Adams left St. Petersburg in 1782, to return to Holland to serve as his father's secretary. Traveling through Stockholm, Sweden and Copenhagen, Denmark, he arrived at Hague, Holland in April 1783. He then returned to Paris, France with his father where he continued to study Latin and to read the English poets. He accompanied his father to London, England in October 1783, and then returned to Holland in January 1784, where his father sought a loan from the Dutch. He returned to England again in May 1784. Adams traveled back to Paris, France where he stayed before he returned to London, England when his father was appointed Ambassador to Great Britain.

Adams returned to the United States in July 1785 to finish his formal education. He was judged deficient in Greek and Latin, and was advised to study privately until he could pass the entrance exams. In 1786, he enrolled at Harvard where he studied mathematics, science and music. In 1787, Adams graduated from Harvard.

Early Career

After graduating from Harvard, Adams studied law at Newburyport. He studied Blackstone's *Commentaries on the Laws of England*, Hume's *History of England*, Gibbon's *History of the Decline and Fall of the Roman Empire*, and Rousseau's *Confessions*. In 1790, Adams began to practice law at Boston, Massachusetts.

In 1791, Adams began to publish essays in the Boston newspaper *Columbian Centinel* in which he attacked demagoguery and the doctrine of popular infallibility. He also worked as a member of a committee that was responsible for the improvement of the Boston police system. He fought against restrictions of theatrical productions, which had been banned by the Massachusetts Legislature. In particular, he defended dramatic stage performances by writing essays in the *Columbian Centinel*.

Between 1793 and 1794, Adams wrote a series of essays in the *Columbian Centinel* and attacked the French who were arming American privateers for the purpose of raiding English ships. He called these actions highway robbery done under the guise of political villainy; he also defended the power of the President to act against such actions as being implicitly granted by the Constitution.

Diplomatic Career

Because of his essays that he published in the Columbia Centinel, Adams got the attention of President George Washington. As a result, President Washington appointed Adams as America's Minister to the Netherlands in 1794. He set sail for Holland aboard the vessel *Alfred* and arrived at Deal, England in October 1794, from where Adams traveled by land for the remainder of the journey. Adams served as Minister to Holland from 1794 to 1797. During a mission to England in July 1797, he married Louisa Catherine Johnson.

When his father became President in 1797, he appointed Adams as the American representative to the Court of the King of Prussia in Berlin. Adams left Holland in October 1797, to travel to Hamburg, and arrived at Berlin in November 1797. During his time as Minister to Berlin between 1797 to 1801, Adams immersed himself in the German language, especially with German poets and philosophers. In April 1801, Adams found out that his father had recalled him and he left Berlin in June 1801. He returned aboard the *America* to Philadelphia in September 1801, and then returned to Boston, Massachusetts to resume his practice of law.

United States Senator

Adams was elected as a state senator in April 1802. In July 1802, Adams lost his appointment as commissioner of bankruptcy when President Jefferson removed all federal office incumbents that were left from the previous administration. Adams then decided to run for Representative in 1802, but he lost the election. When the incumbent United States Senators from Massachusetts announced that they no longer wished to continue in office, the opportunity became available for Adams to run for one of these positions. In 1803, the Massachusetts State Legislature elected Adams as United States Senator.

Adams assumed his post as Senator in October 1803. Adams was on a committee that was responsible for recommending a treaty with England, the Convention of 1803, which was selected for the purpose of assigning the northwest boundary between the United States and Canada. Because the boundary had been moved further south than was designated in the original agreement, Adams urged the Senate to repudiate that portion of the proposed treaty. When England saw this objection, she refused to proceed further in the talks, thus leaving the boundary question unresolved.

Adams pushed for a Constitutional Amendment to justify the Louisiana Purchase. He also argued that the citizens of the Louisiana Territory should have the right to create their own government. Congress ignored his suggestions and imposed a constitution and a tax system upon Louisiana. In 1807, Adams was on a committee that was charged with considering an embargo to prohibit exports from all American ports by any ships. Adams recommended the measure on the grounds that the United States was obligated to defend its rights as a neutral nation, and because he believed that this was a better way to deal with the issue—rather than going to war. He also introduced a bill to exclude British commerce from American ports.

His support of the embargo created much opposition to him in Massachusetts. In 1808, the Massachusetts Legislature voted on whether to replace his seat before the end of his term in February 1809. In an ultimatum, the legislature directed Adams to vote for the repeal of the embargo. Adams refused the instruction, and instead he resigned from the Senate.

Minister to Russia

In March 1809, President James Madison appointed Adams as the American Minister to Russia. He departed aboard the *Horace* and reached St. Petersburg in October 1809, where he began his assignment at the court of the Czar of Russia. From this post, Adams was able to report on the events of Europe, including the French emperor Napoleon's invasion of Russia. This European experience made him a supporter of the policy of isolation of the United States from the wars of European politics.

In 1810, Adams was considered by President Madison for Supreme Court Justice. When Associate Justice William Cushing died in September 1810, President Madison appointed Adams to fill the vacancy, but Adams declined the position.

When the War of 1812 broke out between Britain and the United States, the Czar of Russia attempted to act as a mediator. His efforts were rejected by England, and eventually Adams was called to serve as one of the three envoys in the peace negotiations at Ghent in March 1814. Adams and the other envoys were able to reach an agreement with England that resulted in the Treaty of Ghent.

Minister to England

In May 1815, Adams was appointed by President Madison to serve as Minister of the United States to England. His duties consisted largely of greeting American visitors, issuing passports, looking after commercial matters, and attending dinners, balls and receptions. Adams served in this position until 1817, when he was appointed by President Monroe to be Secretary of State. He sailed from England aboard the *Washington* and arrived at New York City in August 1817.

Secretary of State

Adams arrived in Washington, D.C. to begin his new career as Secretary of State—an office that he held until 1825. As Secretary of State, Adams pursued the guiding principles that he had practiced in Europe, and he helped to crystallize the foundations of American foreign policy. In his first action, he addressed the unanswered questions between England and the United States that remained from the signing of the Treaty of Ghent. Through the Treaty of 1818, Adams was able to have the boundary between the United States and Britain be established at the 49th parallel.

Another of his diplomatic achievements was the the Adams-Onis Treaty with Spain that was signed in 1819. By working with the Spanish Representative to the United States, Adams produced an agreement by which Spain acknowledged East Florida and West Florida to be a part of the United States. Spain also agreed to a boundary extending from the Gulf of Mexico to the Rocky Mountains and along the 42nd parallel to the Pacific Ocean, and agreed to give up any claims to the Oregon Territory. The idea of drawing the boundary through to the Pacific Ocean in the Spanish treaty was the inspiration of Adams—an action that has been referred to as the greatest diplomatic victory ever won by a single individual in the history of the United States.

Adams deferred the recognition of the independence of the new states of Spanish America until the Adams-Onis Treaty had been ratified. When the Senate approved the treaty, President Monroe then recognized Colombia, Mexico, Chile, the United Provinces of the Rio de la Plata, and later Brazil and the Confederation of Central America.

Adams did not get involved with the Missouri Compromise of 1820. Still, he saw the future of the Union and the dignity of humanity as prime issues. Grudgingly, he supported the compromise through a belief that it would preserve the Union until the North would prevail and eventually destroy the slave system.

In February 1821, Adams finished a report on the regulations and standards for weights and measures. His exhaustive research on weighing and measuring entitled *Report of the Secretary of State Upon Weights and Measures* recommended the French metric system as a universal arrangement. However, Congress chose not to implement this.

In 1823, Adams insisted in cabinet meetings that the United States issue a warning to the European powers that the Western Hemisphere was no longer available for conquest, and that they should steer clear of independence movements in Latin America. Although Adams advised that the policy be announced through diplomatic channels, President Monroe chose instead to deliver it as part of his annual address to the Congress in December 1823. The principles that Monroe announced were mostly derived from Adams, and it represented one of the finest contributions to the emergence of the United States as a world power.

Election of 1824

With sectionalism and factionalism developing rapidly, each political group put up its own candidate for the Presidency. Adams was the candidate of the North, while General Andrew Jackson was popular in the South. On the other hand, William Crawford was the choice of the Congressional caucus while Clay was the favorite of the West, the section of the country that wanted higher tariffs and federal support for the development of roads, canals and manufacturing.

Jackson won the popular election with over 152,000 votes as compared to Adams with a little over 114,000 votes. In terms of electoral votes, Jackson also received the most with 99, followed by Adams with 84, Crawford with 41 and Clay with 37. Since no candidate received a majority of Electoral votes, the election was thrown into the House for it to decide among the top 3 candidates. Since Henry Clay was not included, he threw his support of the 3 states that he had won to Adams—mainly because Adams favored a similar internal development program that Clay did.

In a single ballot, the House voted in February 1825, and gave Adams the necessary margin of 13 states, with Jackson getting 7, and Crawford getting 4.

The Term of John Quincy Adams

Events: 1825

<u>March 1825</u>

- In his Inaugural Address President Adams mentioned that after 36 years as a Union, the population had increased to 48,000,000 since the time of the American Revolution, and that much territory had been acquired. He mentioned the evils that had been caused by war, the conflicts that were that were threatening to dissolve the Union, and his belief that in spite of all this, the harmony of the Union should be placed ahead of any party considerations. President Adams announced his intentions to continue with internal improvements, for a national university, and for government-financed projects in science and the arts that were intended for the betterment of the people.
- The members of President Adams' cabinet were as follows:
  - Henry Clay as Secretary of State
  - Richard Rush as Secretary of the Treasury
  - James Barbour as Secretary of War. In 1828, Barbour resigned as Secretary of War and Peter B. Porter replaced him.
  - Samuel L. Southard as Secretary of the Navy
  - John McLean as Postmaster General
  - William Wirt as Attorney General.

- The Mexican state of Texas-Coahuila was declared open to American settlers.

<u>July 1825</u>

- Construction was started to extend the Cumberland Road through Ohio.

<u>October 1825</u>

- The Erie Canal was completed. It linked New York City with the Great Lakes via the Hudson and Mohawk Rivers.

<u>December 1825</u>

- President Adams addressed the Congress and proposed a national program of internal improvements and reforms, including the establishment of a national university, support of the arts and sciences and the creation of a national observatory in Washington, D.C.

Events: 1826

<u>January 1826</u>

- The House proposed adding 4 more circuit courts to the existing 7 that already existed.

<u>February 1826</u>

- The Senate considered a bill to construct a canal through Florida between the Atlantic Ocean and the Gulf of Mexico.

<u>June 1826</u>

- The United States awarded a contract for preliminary expenses to investigate the possibility of constructing a canal across the Isthmus of Central America.

<u>December 1826</u>

- The House inquired into the possibility of establishing a line of communication across the Isthmus of Panama.

Events: 1827

<u>January 1827</u>

- The House proposed an exploration of the Polar Regions.

<u>February 1827</u>

- The Supreme Court ruled in the case of *Martin v. Mott* that the President of the United States has the final power to mobilize the state militia if it is in the national interest.
- The House passed a tariff bill for higher duties on woolen goods, but the Senate rejected the bill.

<u>March 1827</u>

- President Adams issued a proclamation that American ports were closed to trade with the British colonies in retroaction to the British ban on American vessels in British ports.
- The Supreme Court ruled in the case of *Ogden v. Saunders* that a contract made after the passage of a bankruptcy law is controlled by the provisions of that law.
- The House rejected a bill to found a naval academy—a bill that had been narrowly passed by the Senate.

- The United States and Great Britain signed a treaty that extended the agreement of 1818 between them to continue the joint occupation of the Oregon Territory.

December 1827

- President Adams addressed the Congress and emphasized the need for economy in the appropriation of public funds.
- The House defeated a resolution to sell the stock of the Bank of the United States because of concerns that the bank represented a form of monopoly advantage.

Events: 1828

January 1828

- The United States signed a treaty with Mexico that set the common boundary between them along the Sabine River.
- The Senate passed a bill to abolish imprisonment as a punishment for unpaid debts.

February 1828

- The House considered the retrenchment of government funding as a means of cutting expenses.

March 1828

- The House passed a bill that approved appropriations for internal improvements.
- The House rejected a bill to authorize the expedition of the polar regions of the earth.
- The Senate refused to consider a bill to explore the coast of the American Northwest.

May 1828

- President Adams signed The Tariff passed by Congress.
- Congress passed the Reciprocity Law that nullified all discriminatory import duties on trade with reciprocating nations.

December 1828

- Andrew Jackson was elected as President by receiving 183 Electoral votes.
- The House considered a bill to authorize the occupation of the Oregon River in the American Northwest.

Events: 1829

<u>January 1829</u>

- The House considered an appropriation to conduct an exploration of the Southern Hemisphere.
- The House considered a bill to divide the Michigan Territory into two parts: a Michigan Territory and a Huron Territory.
- The House proposed a canal between the Mississippi River and Lake Pontchartrain in the state of Louisiana.

<u>March 1829</u>

- Andrew Jackson was inaugurated as President by being sworn in by Chief Justice John Marshall.

Later Years

In 1829, Adams returned to Massachusetts to enjoy his farm and his books. In 1830, the 12th District of Massachusetts elected him to the House of. Adams took his seat as a Representative in 1831. As chairman of the Committee on manufacturing, he became involved in the two main issues that were being addressed by Congress: the lowering of tariff rates and whether to keep the national bank in existence. He wanted to create a protective tariff that would spur economic growth, and he was in favor of keeping the national bank because he thought that it was an important institution to make America into a powerful nation.

In 1833, Adams was nominated for Governor of Massachusetts, which he declined. He resumed his fight against the circumscription of civil liberties. He served again as Chairman of the Committee on manufacturing from where he opposed patronage policies and defended the government structure of separation of powers.

Adams favored the creation of a federal institution that would be devoted to scholarship. In 1835, James Smithson had bequeathed $500,000 to the United States for the establishment of a learned institution to increase the knowledge among its citizens. Adams offered a motion in the House that the gift be referred to a committee—of which he became the chairman. Smithson's vision for America prevailed as a result of Adams buying bonds and averting the use of these funds for personal projects by other Congressmen—actions that led to the formation of the Smithsonian Institute.

In 1836, Adams returned to the House to enter the debate over the admission of Texas into the Union. In 1844, his allies in the Senate defeated a treaty that would have annexed Texas. However, in 1845, the Texas republic was annexed to the United States by a joint resolution of Congress.

In 1842, his opponents tried to censure Adams, but the House failed to pass the censure motion by defeating it. In 1846, Adams and his associates were overwhelmed by a vote of 176 members of the House who approved a resolution that authorized President James Polk to conduct a war against Mexico. In 1847, Adams recovered from various afflictions to to attend the House sessions. His last work was devoted to improving the new observatory that was located in Washington, D.C.

In February 21, 1848, Adams collapsed on the floor of the House from a stroke. He was carried to the Speaker's private chamber, where he lingered for 2 days. On February 23, 1848, John Quincy Adams died at the age of 80.

Legacy

Adams' policy was to exert national power to make freedom more fruitful for the people. He was guided by an aspiration to lead the civilized nations into a noble agreement to reduce belligerent activities and thus to promote a better environment for humanity. Thus, he supported the Bank of the United States as an instrument of the national fiscal authority, and a national tariff to protect domestic industries. During his administration the public debt was reduced from $16,000,000 to only $5,000,000. In foreign affairs, 9 commercial treaties were concluded.

Adams also fought for a broad national program of internal physical improvements to create and to maintain highways, canals, and railways. In the field of education, he favored the development of science as well as geographical discoveries although his stance on these issues was ahead of his times.

Transformation of the Presidency

Synopsis of Change

In the first 40 years of its Constitutional existence, the first presidents under the Constitution established the office with respect to its scope, power and extent. Through their combined actions these men created precedents for dealing with contingencies that were beyond the constraints and rules as stated in the Constitution. Through their combined actions, the Constitution of the United States was transformed from a mere document into a living and powerful agreement that served to guide a strong—but free—central government.

Legacy of the First 6 Presidents

The executive power has been used since the time of the first 6 Presidents—and further expanded—to handle events and circumstances that were not anticipated by the founders of the Constitution. In foreign affairs, many wars, depressions, disasters, civil strife, illicit commerce (such as the trafficking of drugs and weapons), and other calamitous events have occurred. These events have forced the President to sometimes act beyond the scope that the original founders of the country envisioned as necessary to protect and maintain the proper functioning of government. The changing nature of the world, especially with the rise and fall of nations, have changed the limits of foreign policy actions to accommodate the multifaceted situations of dealing with other world leaders—including that of unilateral actions. The President has even resorted to military police actions in reaction to events that have been deemed as threatening to our internal security or adverse to our national interests.

In domestic affairs, troops have been called by the President to quell local disturbances, to assist in disasters, and to enforce martial law whenever it has been imposed. The economic powers have been expanded to include the calling of financial holidays, the power to freeze assets within financial institutions, and even the unmitigated power to hold back federal funds for projects or programs that a President is not in favor of conducting. As a role model the President has acted to persuade a change in social attitudes, especially with regard to discriminatory policies instituted by state and local governments. In gridlock battles with the Congress, the President has often appealed to the public to gain support for policies that are intended for the major good and general welfare. In security matters, the protection for a President has increased dramatically with the advent of new invasive technology, the easy availability of weapons, the increased danger of being assassinated in public, and the threat from foreign agents and rogue nations.

The expansions of power were implicitly granted in the Constitution under the vague clause outlining the duties of the executive branch. However, all that the Constitution states is that the executive power will be vested in the President. It was the first 6 Presidents who instituted policies and took actions that were beyond the law, and in the process it was they who defined the office for their successors. But, they did so in a way that preserved the democratic intent of the framers of the Constitution. Were it not for their prophetic insight and attention to the future in setting the precedents for the office, the direction of the country could easily have gone along a very different path. The United States is truly blessed that in its formative years it had as Presidents 6 of the best American citizens of the time—*and possibly of all time*.

Bibliography

Adler, Mortimer J., Editor in Chief. *The Annals of America*, Vol. 3-10. Chicago: Encyclopaedia Britannica, Inc., 1976.

Hargreaves, Mary W. M. *The Presidency of John Quincy Adams*. Lawrence: University Press of Kansas, 1985.

Ketcham, Ralph. *James Madison: A Biography*. Charlottesville: University Press of Virginia, 1990.

McCullough, David. *John Adams*. New York: Simon and Schuster, 2001.

Randall, Willard Sterne. *Thomas Jefferson: A Life*. New York: Harper Perennial, 1993.

_____. *George Washington: A Life*. New York: Henry Holt and Company, 1997.

Unger, Harlow Giles. *The Last Founding Father: James Monroe and a Nation's Call to Greatness*. Boston: De Capo Press, 2010.

Made in the USA
Las Vegas, NV
02 May 2025

21616082R00063